Among the Bankers

Among the Bankers

A JOURNEY INTO THE HEART
OF FINANCE

Joris Luyendijk

MELVILLE HOUSE
BROOKLYN · LONDON

Among the Bankers

First Melville House Printing: September 2016

Melville House Publishing   8 Blackstock Mews
          46 John Street   and   Islington
        Brooklyn, NY 11201   London N4 2BT

mhpbooks.com   facebook.com/mhpbooks   @melvillehouse

Design by Marina Drukman

ISBN: 978-1-61219-591-9

Printed in the United States of America
1   3   5   7   9   10   8   6   4   2

A catalog record for this book is available from
the Library of Congress

For the late Gerd Baumann,
who taught me that curiosity will do

'The real conspiracy in the financial sector is the sounds of silence.'

PHILIP AUGAR,
The Greed Merchants, 2005

Contents

Introduction

You're on a plane. The seatbelt signs have been switched off, you have just been given your drink and now you are trying to decide between the in-flight entertainment and your book. The man next to you is quietly sipping his whiskey, while you gaze absently through the window at the sun and the clouds. Suddenly you see a gigantic flash of fire coming out of one of the engines. You call the flight attendant. Yes, she says, there were some technical difficulties but it's all under control. She looks so composed and confident that you almost believe her. But you get up, unable to contain your alarm. First the relaxed flight attendant and then an officious cabin manager try to stop you as you make your way towards the front of the plane. Sir, please go back to your seat. You push them aside, grab the cockpit door, manage to open it and . . . there is nobody there.

The past few years I have spoken to around 200 people who work or have recently worked in the financial district of London. Their stories are very different but if I were to summarise them in one image, it would be that empty cockpit.

•

This project grew out of one fundamental question: why many people seem to have so little *interest* in issues that directly affect their *interests*. Is it indifference and apathy, or have many subjects simply become too complicated for outsiders to understand? To find out, I had launched an experiment for a Dutch newspaper. I had taken an important, complicated and apparently boring issue that I knew nothing about – sustainable transportation – and asked a beginner's question: are electric cars a good idea? I had put this to an insider, whose answers led to new questions, which prompted interviews with other insiders and so on until a sort of 'learning curve' of articles and stories had come about. Insiders were happy to make time while readers seemed to appreciate it when you started from zero.

So in 2011 when the *Guardian* asked me to compile such a 'learning curve,' about the City, the 2008 global financial collapse, and its ongoing effects, I was intrigued. I understood as little of the world of finance as the average reader and this was a perfect example of an issue with a huge gap between the public interest and the interest of the public. Tell someone their money is not safe and you have their full attention; say the words 'financial reforms' and people switch off.

Only a few years ago the City—like its U.S. equivalent, Wall Street—had seen the biggest financial panic since the 1930s. Billions and billions had been spent to bail out the industry yet nobody had gone to prison. Indeed, a few years on, the bankers seemed to be behaving more and more as if it were 'business as usual' again. I happily assented to write the column, hopeful that the paper's prestige would gain me access to famously secretive financial industry insiders.

That's how a Dutch journalist with five years' experience in the Middle East and a degree in anthropology ended up in the City on an unusual investigation: Tintin among the bankers.

Among the Bankers

1

Behind the Wall of Silence

When looking into the pros and cons of the electric car I had started from zero, without doing any research. Adopting a beginner's outlook had forced insiders to use simple language and I figured I'd try that approach again for this project.

Now I just needed that beginner's question. I asked friends and acquaintances in Amsterdam and London what they wanted to know about the world of finance. Almost everyone I spoke to was angry without being able to explain exactly why. Nobody seemed to understand what had actually happened during the collapse of the American bank Lehman Brothers in 2008 or the ensuing crash, the biggest financial panic since the 1930s. I kept hearing, 'If you can help me understand how it works in finance then I'll be grateful. But I know that within two days I will have forgotten all that technical stuff again.'

All right, I would respond. Is there a question about finance or bankers that occupies you so much that you *would* remember the answer? These were difficult conversations because people needed to vent their outrage first. 'Isn't it incredible,' they would say, 'that we had to bail out these bankers and yet none of them have had to pay back their bonuses? Look at how the cuts hit the most vulnerable in society. Meanwhile bankers give themselves huge bonuses, even at banks that exist only because we saved them.' Eventually it occurred to me that my friends were asking the same thing: 'How can these people live with themselves?' That seemed a good start – phrased a bit more subtly, perhaps.

As soon as I had settled in London I got out my address book and approached everyone I knew, asking them to introduce me to someone who worked in the City. Responses would take a while to come in, of course, giving me the chance to explore my new home in the meantime. I had always thought of London in the same category as Berlin and Paris: the capital of a big European country. But London is the size of Berlin, Madrid and Paris *put together*.

I took the tube into the centre of town and went for a walk. Now I could begin to see for myself that 'the City' as a term is no longer accurate. The financial sector in London employs between 250,000 and 300,000 people. That is a lot of jobs and they have begun to spread across the capital. To the west near Piccadilly Circus lies the well-heeled and discreet area of Mayfair, where you'll find the more adventurous types of professional investors of other people's money: private equity and hedge funds as well as venture capitalists. Then there is the historical 'City' or 'Square Mile' near Bank tube station, where many brokerage firms, the insurance sector and a number of big banks such as Goldman Sachs are surrounded by architectural icons such as St Paul's Cathedral, the Bank of England and the illustrious former Stock Exchange (now a restaurant and shopping centre). Moving east towards City Airport you reach Canary Wharf, a former harbour where increasing numbers of banks and financial institutions have their headquarters. Canary Wharf is made up of seductively shiny glass skyscrapers and a huge shopping centre, fringed by manicured greenery, each corner observed by the constant gaze of CCTV cameras. The area is privately owned and privately controlled, as any activists who gather to protest are swiftly informed – every piece of land on Canary Wharf apart from the 50 yards outside the Jubilee Line station is private.

Several days passed while I continued wandering around the city. I hadn't had a single response to my request for introductions to financial insiders. I was beginning to worry when a friend I knew from Jerusalem invited me to a party where he introduced me to 'Sid.' Sid was in his late thirties, tall and broad-shouldered, the son of immigrants. After a career as a trader with a number of major banks he had joined a few colleagues to start a brokerage firm: a company that buys and sells products in the markets on behalf of clients for a commission. Helping outsiders understand the City was 'more than overdue,' Sid said in a welcoming voice. Why didn't I come over and spend a day at his firm? The only condition was that I could not identify him or his company by name. 'Clients wouldn't understand we're talking to the press.'

A week later, soon after daybreak, I arrived at Sid's firm on a busy street in the historical heart of the City. Sid had already told me that there is a clear divide in the world of finance between those who see their children in the morning and those who see them in the evening. The ones who work in tandem with 'the markets' have to get up really, really early to be ready to go when the markets open. They see their children in the evening. The other part of the financial world works independently of the markets, for instance lawyers and dealmakers in mergers and acquisitions. They can take their children to nursery or school, but work late pretty much every evening. When you see financial workers having lunch somewhere in the City, it's always this second category. People who work with the markets have their lunches next to their computer screens.

'Why don't you find something to do for a moment?' Sid suggested. 'I need to finish my note to investors before half seven.' He walked over to his desk where an impressive array of computer screens showed news tickers, graphs and market data. Everywhere I looked there were telephones and TVs switched to the financial news channels. There was less than an hour to go before the markets opened; an atmosphere of concentrated anticipation filled the room. My stomach tensed like it does before a crucial World Cup game.

Sid explained that his note consisted of analysis and invest-ment advice for his clients: mostly pension funds, insurance companies and other professional investors of other people's money. He estimated that his clients received at least 300 such emails each day. 'I try to be short and to the point – clients' attention span will never exceed a page. The best you can hope for is that they read a few paragraphs.' In his notes he did not make statements on individual companies – there were whole teams of researchers for that elsewhere, he said. Instead he went for what he described as 'the bird's-eye view of the entire econ-omy.' For the rest of the day he offered commentary on new developments and updated his note.

Was he like a sports commentator, with the markets being the match? He thought for a moment. 'Maybe, except my anal-ysis is directed at the coaches and players in the field, rather than the audience in the stadium.' Among his clients were also traders at major banks. 'All of us here have worked at big banks, so we know what it's like there. It can be a pretty lonely life as a trader. You have specialised in one particular area, say the auto-mobile industry. That's your "book." But there may be only one of you with that book. Maybe there's a junior helping you out, but that's it. Our research is like a sounding board for clients, a second opinion. We pass out good ideas but also nuggets of insight that they can use to look good in front of their boss.'

The markets opened and for half an hour everybody seemed extremely busy. Brokers were shouting to each other across the floor: 'Did you see gold at 1670?' As things were settling down, a broker whose job it was to 'go into' the market and find a buyer for what her clients wanted to sell and vice versa kept one eye on the *Sun* and the other on her screens. 'What's the difference between a broker and his client?' she asked me. 'A broker says "fuck you" only *after* hanging up the phone.'

I wrote it down in my notebook and went over to a man in his late twenties with his fingertips against his temples. He was staring at four screens and leaning in so close his nose nearly touched one of them. He explained that he was doing 'technical analysis.' Simplified: he was looking for trends in the share price of a particular set of companies, and gave investment advice on that basis. The markets had captivated him from secondary school onwards. He didn't understand much about economics and he quickly learned that only the big players can pay for the sophisticated and high-value research like Sid's. Then he discovered 'technical analysis,' a way of working with public data to study the market. 'I have been doing this for quite a few years now,' he said, 'and it's surprisingly often about intuition, the unconscious recognition and spotting of patterns.'

'Hey, you,' Sid called out mock-sternly: 'You go talk to our Dutch guest.' And so I sat down with a well-spoken and slightly haggard-looking man in his late twenties. He told me that as a sales guy he considered himself lucky. He only had to get up at 5:30 a.m. whereas people like Sid rose at five. I was taking everything down as fast as I could in my little notebook when the *Sun*-reading broker passed me a folded piece of paper that said: 'Seriously deranged but harmless – most of the time.' With a smile, the sales guy crunched it up and threw it at the broker's head. He shrugged: 'Trading-floor humour.'

His job as 'sales guy' is to take the analysis from Sid or

the technical analyst to his own body of clients in the hope of getting them to buy or sell something through his broker-age. He was a kind of filter, he explained, because he knew his clients' needs very well. Some focused on the psychology of the market of the day and preferred to read technical analysis, others looked at long-term and 'fundamental' aspects such as the actual financial health of a corporation. He pointed to his screen: 'Here, look at my client list. I have been working with these guys for years. Many of them I brought with me when I moved to this company. Clients do business with a person, not only with the firm they work for.' In the end there are two types of salesmen, he said: 'The ones who know how to listen well, and the aggressive ones, who get others to do what they want. The latter often do very well, but as I am generally in the first camp, I hope I can last the distance.'

And did he think he would? He hesitated. 'Currently, I wonder why I am doing this. The hours are terrible and the pay can be dreadful for a long time.' He was working on a freelance basis, his pay was commission-based and business had been very slow ever since the crash. Meanwhile his fixed costs were high: financial data subscriptions, telephone systems, PCs with three, four or five screens, treating clients to lunches and nights out . . . 'You have to be very thick-skinned and insanely optimistic about life to get through without too many break-downs, or alcoholism.'

By now, the markets in London and the rest of Europe were closing, finally allowing me a moment to sit back and catch my breath. So this was a small trading floor. What I had seen was part of the 'financial markets,' as in the familiar news reports: 'Financial markets this morning reacted positively to the German election result.' All those numbers on screens appeared to signify an exact and unambiguous universe, but at the same time it felt somewhat illusory, as if it were a computer game without any consequences.

When everybody had finished their digital paperwork, it was time for the pub. Had this been a good day? For the technical analyst it had not: prices had 'behaved' differently from his forecasts: 'Tomorrow is another day.' Sid also looked less than happy. His note had predicted an intervention by the Swiss central bank. 'What was great was that fifteen minutes later, the Swiss central bank did intervene,' he said. 'Less great was that due to a misunderstanding my note didn't go out. Had it gone out, you might say that I would have "scored" with my clients, who would have noticed my prediction coming true.' Another swig of his beer: 'Provided, of course, that they had read my note in the first place.'

•

That day with Sid was the best introduction to the City I could have hoped for, but it was also a stroke of luck. My other requests for interviews had been met with silence, or a rhetorical counter question: why should I invest time to contribute to a better understanding of my sector, when all outsiders want is a reason to hate us? Most responded with a polite yet firm 'no thank you,' no matter how much I grovelled or begged.

I looked up Sid again and over a beer I finally learnt what was going on: the world of finance is governed by a code of silence. Sid and his mates were their own bosses, but employees of banks and other financial firms risk losing their jobs, being sued and suffering severe damage to their reputation if they are caught speaking to the press. Try finding a new job in the City after that. Severance clauses explicitly state that you cannot disclose anything about your experiences at your firm.

For a moment I thought, there goes my 'learning curve.' But intimidation is rarely completely effective. Even in Iraq under Saddam Hussein it was possible for foreign journalists to get people to talk – provided they felt safe. I continued sending out requests for interviews, only this time with additional guarantees and promises: nobody will ever know that we spoke. I am the only one with access to this mailbox and your exact job title, bank or financial firm will never be revealed, nor your nationality or ethnic background.

A new wave of polite rejections followed, until a sales manager for data management services in mergers and acquisitions suddenly said 'sure.' This was shortly followed by a financial lawyer who agreed to have lunch, after which a primary research firm manager, an analyst at a private equity boutique, a banker in mergers and acquisitions and a banker who did corporate finance all agreed to meet me. We would meet incognito, at their homes or some other place where the chance of bumping into colleagues or former colleagues was nil. I like to record interviews but this made people very nervous so everything had to be done using notes. This was one of the reasons I wanted them to sign off on the interview: did I get everything right? I wanted all of them to see the text before it went online. I worried that critical remarks would be scrapped but my fears proved unfounded. It was mostly sentences that had seemed entirely innocuous: 'Please remove that "beautiful view from the ninth floor" otherwise everybody in my niche will know it's me.' Or: 'Don't put in that I am starting the day with a cup of tea. I am the only one on my trading floor who does that!' Some seemed almost ashamed of their nervousness and asked me to take out any references to their anxiety – a code of silence about the code of silence.

As soon as I had ten signed-off interviews I posted them on the *Guardian* blog accompanied by an appeal to insiders to trade anonymity for honesty and to tell us what goes on in those glass towers. 'Democracy is beginning to look like the system by which electorates decide which politician gets to implement what the markets dictate,' I added. 'So who are you?'

And then it happened. Within a few hours my inbox began to fill up. The first 10 interviewees had all been male, but now women came forward, often employed in obscure-sounding jobs: a bond pricer, who determined the value of bonds that were traded so rarely that they have no current market price; an insurance broker, who connected ship owners who want to insure their ships against a range of risks with insurance underwriters who take on those risks in exchange for a premium; an investment management adviser, who helped banks restructure or update their computer systems, for example to keep up with new regulations or technology; a fund raiser at a 'sharia-compliant' venture capital firm who brought together investors and promising entrepreneurs.

In a Pret a Manger on Paternoster Square near St Paul's Cathedral I drank a cup of green tea with the head of marketing at one division of a European bank. In her email she wrote that she was 'happy to demystify' the world that she had been in for over 10 years now. 'Any time during the day is OK as I tend to make my own schedule.' She was in her late thirties, spoke with an immaculate middle-class accent and clearly enjoyed making sarcastic jokes and comments. There are three typical reactions, she said, when people discover where she works, for instance at school when she is picking up her child. 'A disappointed look – "Gee, I thought you did something interesting" – or they declare me *persona non grata*, or they treat me like a cheque book, expecting me to pick up the tab.'

She talked about the exhausting amount of booze you are meant to ingest on the many nights out with clients or colleagues, and the difficulty some men have in dealing with a woman who makes more money than they do. When dating you make concessions, she explained. 'Sometimes eating at a cheaper restaurant, taking a less extravagant holiday, making sure they have money to pay so they don't look like they can't cut it. It's a control thing, I suppose.' This made both of us laugh which seemed a good moment to ask about her own pay-packet. 'You know what, I feel uncomfortable saying that aloud,' she answered, and wrote on a napkin: £110,000. 'Plus bonus,' she added, which typically comes to half her salary, in addition to 20 per cent options. 'When times are good, it can be a lot higher, possibly double.' There was a short silence. 'Let me add that people do give to charity. Most I know donate about 10 per cent of their bonuses, and often they put in time, for instance organising fundraisers. We don't like to talk about it to the outside world, but amongst ourselves, it's a big topic. How much did you give? How much did you raise?' We are spoilt, she conceded. 'Some of my friends are teaching assistants, they make £12k a year . . .' Earlier she had said that her academic background had nothing to do with the financial sector. Why the City, then? Her expression barely altered but something in her voice changed when she answered: 'I needed to bring up my child on my own. That meant I had to find a job that paid double, essentially.'

The head of marketing had not been overly concerned about the code of silence and this made her a real exception. Almost every other interview I conducted took place under a cloud of stress and fear. On more than one occasion an interviewee would suddenly freeze, squeeze their face into a jolly grin, look me straight in the eyes and whisper: 'We are leaving. Now.' A colleague would have come in, perhaps because he or she was using that same discreet coffee place for a clandestine meeting, with a head-hunter for example. At least half the potential interviewees bailed out after the initial contact, simply by no longer responding to my emails. More than once somebody failed to show up, or cancelled with a text message

– sometimes when I was already waiting for them, notebook in hand. A number of people withdrew after the interview, for instance two women who separately wanted to blow the whistle about racism, homophobia and sexual harassment at their brokerage firms. 'Feel really bad saying this and wasting your time,' one of them wrote, 'but having read in black and white what I said to you I just don't feel comfortable with it being published at all and worried it would be career suicide.'

Women were almost without exception more nervous than men, and the latter would sometimes say: 'My wife thinks I'm crazy for doing this.' When I mentioned to women that they seemed so much more anxious, almost all of them reacted with irritation: 'God, I hate it when I behave like a typical woman.' Others said: 'You see? Women are more aware of the risks they are taking.'

'You have no idea how weird this is for me,' said a woman who used to work for the department that everyone else was so afraid of: PR and communication. 'If I were still with the bank we would not be having this conversation.' It was one of those grey and rainy days that often make me homesick for Holland and we were meeting in a nondescript coffee shop somewhere near her home in London. She was in her mid thirties and had recently quit the industry after 10 years at a number of top banks.

So how did her department find out if someone in the bank had spoken to the media? She shrugged: 'There are external agencies that monitor the media for us. Sometimes people in the bank send you stuff: "Look at this."' There would be a hearing, followed by disciplinary measures or dismissal. She described a few cases of bankers who had been caught, adding that they had to teach them that no matter how nice the journalist is, 'he is not your friend.' With a hint of satisfaction she concluded that, at least in her last bank, 'enough people have been disciplined for speaking to unauthorised contacts in the press that it hardly happens any more.'

She went over the rules for 'authorised contacts' via the PR department: the topics are agreed on beforehand and the PR sits in on the interview as witness and referee. Should a journalist veer off the approved topics, it is the job of PR to step in: 'Nice try but he's not gonna answer that.' Or even better: 'He can't answer that but let me try and hook you up later with someone who can.' After the interview the PR 'cleans the quotes,' which is not as sinister as it sounds, she insisted. 'It's about making sure the quotes make sense in context. That if there's something that could be misinterpreted, it's removed.' After all, reputation is among a bank's core assets.

We had another coffee and when she asked if I had ever considered trying my luck in the financial sector, I responded evasively that quite a few journalists seem to do so. She agreed: the pay is much better but those who do make the switch are in for a shock. Earlier we had talked about the abusive culture of top banks. 'The thing is,' she said, amused, 'journalists have no idea what they're in for. I would sometimes come across one who had gone over to our side and he'd have this shell-shocked look. The first six months they are like, *what the fuck?* They had no idea because bankers were always really, really nice to them.'

Now it was my turn to laugh, and I explained that this is why I never do interviews via PRs. She would never have said this if there had been a colleague of hers present as witness and referee, would she? So what made her violate the very rule that for so many years she had enforced on others? She thought for a moment and said she wanted to contribute to a more balanced debate. 'I suppose I spent an entire career not giving my own opinions,' she continued. 'Inside I'd be screaming, "Yes, that's exactly the question you should be asking," only to shut down the journalist and direct the interview back to where the bank wanted it to be. Maybe this is also confession, like a good Catholic.'

•

Just how deep this fear runs is difficult to convey. As the blog took off, academics, journalists and documentary filmmakers enquired whether the same bank employees I had spoken to might be prepared to meet with them. When I passed these requests on, the reply was invariably: 'Sorry, risking my job once is enough.'

This strict code of silence suppresses what outsiders get to see of the City. It couldn't be more different to my electric car assignment. There, insiders were eager to meet me and I was the one who chose who to interview. Now I had to wait for volunteers to come forward to reveal the details of their job and working life. These volunteers took the risk because they wanted to challenge a particular stereotype about the world of finance, the inner workings of the City or their own job – for example, the assumption that all of finance is horribly complicated. Yes, interviewees said, what the maths and physics wizards or quants do is extremely difficult to understand. But the rest of us . . .

'There is a lot of lingo,' explained a man who until recently worked for a big bank in mergers and acquisitions. 'I mean a lot, and you have to master all that. But you don't have to be brilliant to work in finance; you have to be smart enough.' He was around 30 years old, originally from East Asia, and he spoke with the polite imperturbability that many alumni of American elite universities have made their own. Factual errors on my part were countered with: 'Actually, no . . .' An incorrect claim or interpretation was met with: 'I think I'd challenge the premise in what you just said.'

A career in the City is in part 'endurance sport,' he said, and others agreed. The head of marketing who preferred not to say out loud how much she made insisted that many had more or less drifted into the sector. Anyone can do the job I'm doing, she said. 'Sure, sometimes you need to be trained on some of the technical stuff. But at my first job interview I didn't even know the difference between equity and bonds. What you need is self-belief.'

We are not all rocket scientists, interviewees said, and we are certainly not all millionaires. An interdealer broker with many years' experience on a trading floor spoke for many when he said: 'The sad reality in finance is that perhaps 5 per cent really make a lot of money. The rest do make more than those with similar levels of education in other industries. But they also put in longer hours. How it works, I suppose, is that I am at my desk and I look at my boss. He has millions in the bank, his own jet, a few cars, a hotel in the Mediterranean . . . and I wonder. My boss is not that much smarter than I am. Still, he has all this money. Why him and not me? So I sign on for another year, waiting for the big one. That's the thing with the City. The 95 per cent know that only a small percentage make the huge sums. But you are exposed to that category of people, every day and up close. It plants the idea in your head: this could be me.'

'It's just a normal office environment,' said an internal accountant at a big British bank when I asked her what would be most surprising for outsiders to learn about her job. 'Normal people,' she went on. 'Not loud. Not arrogant. And not overpaid, at least not us. If I found a similar job in another industry, I'd make maybe 10 per cent less. At most.' When she began working as an accountant she was advised to start at a bank; after that you could go anywhere. But this was before the crisis. For some time now she had been trying to find a job away from financial services. Her recruitment consultant found a vacancy that seemed perfect for her and her experience. She was the only person on the shortlist who was not invited for interview; the company did not think someone from a bank would fit into their culture, they had told her recruitment consultant. 'They'd never met me,' she said bitterly, 'and made assumptions about my character purely based on where I currently work.' On dating sites these days you'd better hide that you're working in a bank, she added. 'Or you'll have no chance.' Many interviewees said that when meeting new people at parties or at the school gates, they had learnt to keep where they worked to themselves, fearing negative reactions.

As each interviewee set me straight on clichés about the world of finance, I also began to learn new things – first that the sector is far larger than the banks and second about the deep divide between investment bankers and those in retail or commercial banking. As one commercial banker put it: 'If investment bankers are hunters who go out in search of prey, commercial are like farmers patiently tilling the land.'

A young restructurer who tried to prevent companies in financial difficulties from going bankrupt – and defaulting on the loans his (retail) bank had made to them – emphasised a number of times how his work was different from investment banking. He had spent some time there, on a trading floor. He compared it unfavourably with his current environment: 'There is quite a lot of camaraderie among restructuring teams. And no ceremony. It's not like at some investment banks where as a junior you can't take something to a senior managing director. No one's bigger than the team, we say, and everyone takes turns getting coffee.'

Or consider the woman who wrote in her email: 'The more traditional side of banking – making actual loans – is seriously under-represented on your blog.' So a little while later we met for lunch in a restaurant on the Thames. It was the Christmas holidays and the City had changed beyond recognition. The well-dressed men and women purposefully hurrying to their next appointment were gone, replaced by shivering tourists in bright outfits. My interviewee was in her late twenties, English, with a science background. She ordered French toast with strawberries and dug into them with gusto.

The City sees my kind of banking as dull, she said dismissively. 'But traders sit in their glass buildings all day shouting into their phones and staring at a screen, turning one number into another. I help build schools, toll roads, bridges, oil rigs and power plants in faraway places. I travel all over Europe, to Russia, Asia and Saudi Arabia, on my own, to inaugurate a gas plant, open a solar park or inspect an oil refinery. Now, who has the boring job? The world of banking is so much bigger than the dealmakers and traders who dominate the public's idea of us. That is my message,' she said, 'to readers but also to my family and friends who seem to think that I caused the crash by hunting for a monster bonus.'

The area she had been working in for the past decade or so was called 'project finance.' A government wants a school, bridge, power plant or airport built. It puts the project out to tender, meaning firms can bid for the contract. Different parties come together because no single company has all the required expertise. A construction company knows how to build a school, but not how to operate it, nor how to finance it, she explained. She loved it. 'Most people in finance work on a small part of a deal, pass it on to someone else, who again does a bit, then hands it over, and so on. We do the whole thing, and when I drive through the country, I think to myself, "Ha, that's my toll road, that's my school, that's my police station." This is so fulfilling.'

Like the restructurer, she had interned at an investment

bank for a brief period, processing trades. 'I'd get shouted at all the time, often for things that *they* had done wrong. A good trader needs to be very assertive and to have a very quick response. That attitude carries over into their interactions with other people. You'll find them screaming at the sandwich lady in the canteen.' In project finance, she makes around £100,000 a year, which she considered 'grossly overpaid, in the greater scheme of things.' She refused to feel guilty though, she said, because she pays her full share in taxes. Surely with her experience, contacts and talent for maths she could make far more in an investment bank? No thanks, she said. 'Investment banks make money with money, they speculate. That creates an atmosphere that I don't find pleasant at all.' She was very happy that her own bank was purely commercial: 'It's a much nicer environment if you don't even have to meet those people in the lift.'

The City, I began to realise, is only human. In all its unwritten rules, dress codes and internal hierarchies, it resembles a village, or a collection of tribes. Insiders identify one another via a subtle system of codes and mores, as a competition lawyer in mergers and acquisitions explained to me. We ate lunch in a soberly decorated restaurant called L'Anima near Exchange Square, a large cluster of offices within the Square Mile. Conservatively dressed and in early middle age, the lawyer looked down the menu and commented in an easy, half-ironic tone: 'Look, they explain all the culinary terms in a separate column under the heading "definitions." That is so lawyer-like. Large contracts often start out with definitions.' He ordered fish and sparkling water: 'I still want to get some work done this afternoon.'

He looked around at the other tables: 'Mostly lawyers here. I see no trophy wives or girlfriends, no extravagantly dressed women. I see men who keep their jackets on, which is what we tend to do as lawyers – nobody wants to be the first to take it off and most leave it on anyhow. Keeping the uniform intact makes you look solid. I see inconspicuous ties, also a lawyer thing. This restaurant serves very good quality food but it is not flashy; I believe only this week the *Sunday Times* called the interior "boring." Boring is good, for lawyers. We sell reliability, solidity and caution. We want our presentation to mirror that.

'Those in the City doing one-time deals tend to project an image of absolute success,' he went on. 'Say you are an entrepreneur looking for a banker to take your company public: to list it on the stock market in a so-called Initial Public Offering or IPO. The only thing that counts is for this deal to go well, not whether the banker executing it charges a 1.2 or a 1.3 per cent fee. The bankers that take companies public will drive the most expensive car they can find because they want the entrepreneur to think: "Wow, this banker must be really good at IPOs, how else could he afford such a car?" Long-term relationships in the City work very differently. When you bill clients by the hour, you leave that expensive watch at home. We often charge hefty fees,' the lawyer explained. 'So we don't flash our wealth because then clients are going to think: "Wait, am I not paying too much?"'

I learnt to not only read ties but shoes and rings too. Bankers from mainland Europe on a visit to the City can be recognised by their brown shoes. Dealmakers like to wear Hermès ties but traders do not. And math wizards who never need to see clients could be extremely successful in their jobs while looking like 'they are dressed by their mum' – as an insider who was clearly not gifted at maths put it. I quickly taught myself to speak of 'Goldman' or 'Goldmans' rather than Goldman Sachs, of 'SocGen' (*sokdzjèn*) for the French bank Société Générale and of 'Deutsche' without the 'Bank.' Corporations are the *real economy* and salary plus bonus is *total comp*. I no longer thought of Tolkien when someone earnestly spoke the words: 'I work in the magic circle' (the nickname for the five law firms dominating the City). A bonus of zero is a *doughnut*, a *broker's ear* the ability to follow five conversations around you at the same time, while the *fat finger syndrome* is every trader's nightmare: things move so fast in the markets that there are no such things as neat little cautionary pop-ups asking, 'Are you sure you want to buy 500,000 shares in British Airways?' A *fat finger* is that fatal moment when you type one zero too many and you have to work like a maniac to limit the damage.

It is not impossibly difficult to learn *Financialese*, and soon enough I could repeat insider jokes. What would a banker at Goldman do if he had five million dollars? Ask what had happened to the rest. There are three kinds of economists: those who can add up and those who can't. Economists correctly predicted seven out of the last three crises. Half of economics is actually very useful – too bad economists can never agree which half.

It was good fun, this first reconnaissance mission. But there remained just one *tiny* problem and my very first interviewee illustrated it as well as anyone. It was a warm summer evening and we were meeting in a French restaurant at Covent Garden, at his suggestion. The place was filled with exhausted tourists giving orders to equally worn-down waiters. My interviewee was a big and easy-going guy, around 25 years old, who had worked for the past few years as sales manager for data management services in mergers and acquisitions. I asked if I could report what he was having, and that was fine: foie gras for starters, followed by a hamburger with fries and for dessert a double macchiato with brandy. We shared a bottle of white wine that he chose. Our appetisers arrived and I opened up my notebook to ask what a sales manager for data management services in mergers and acquisitions actually does.

He took a big bite of foie gras and explained that when a

company is put up for sale, bankers, accountants, consultants and lawyers need to go through its books to determine its value. This can easily take six months to a year, as a company's records are not always well organised. Some are so confidential that a company will keep them as a physical document in a highly secured room. His firm collected and organised all this material to put it on one disc, so the specialists could get to work. 'The CD we compile is of course encrypted,' he said. 'Still, you really don't want to lose that.'

I asked about the biggest taboo in his job, the worst possible misstep for someone like him. He didn't hesitate: 'Breaching confidentiality. The other day I was in this bar when at a table next to mine somebody was discussing a deal in progress, out loud and in detail. If I had acted on what I heard there, that guy would have been fucked. This is one reason we invent codenames for deals. Cartoon characters, Greek gods or anagrams, when they rearrange the letters of a company's name to form a new word. I enjoy thinking about these very expensive and busy and important bankers convening a meeting to brainstorm about a codename.'

He saw my expression and grinned, but then I changed the subject and asked about the crash of 2008. He gave me a blank stare, shrugged his shoulders and said: 'Well, uhh, I don't know. I mean, what do you want me to say? I am in mergers and acquisitions.'

That was the tiny problem.

2

Planet Finance and the Crash

It was an almost inevitable mistake, for a beginner. I had thought of the financial world as essentially a single entity, in which everyone was basically the same. So I'd spread my net far and wide; if the sector as a whole was behind the crash, then everyone working there seemed worth interviewing.

This broad approach helped build my first impressions of the City. But questions like 'how can you live with yourself?' and asking interviewees about their responsibility for the crash aroused responses that came close to hilarity. If they had not already volunteered to make the point that someone with their job had *nothing* to do with the crash, interviewees pointed out that their understanding of '2008' came from the media and from books by journalists. Some people were strikingly ignorant about the crash, and a few even seemed indifferent – for example the foie-gras fan in data management services.

It was becoming increasingly clear that my beginner's phase was over; even more so because by now I had heard stories that scared the hell out of me. The crash may have been as much of a surprise to the interviewees as it was to the rest of the world, but unlike outsiders they did understand the stakes.

They talked about the hours, days and weeks after the Lehman Brothers' collapse on September 15 as the most harrowing period in their careers, if not lives. They spoke of colleagues sitting frozen before their screens, paralysed, unable to act even at moments when there was easy money to be made. Things were looking so bad, they said, that some got on the phone to their families: 'Get as much money from the ATM as you can.' 'Rush to the supermarket to hoard food.' 'Buy gold.' 'Get everything ready to evacuate the kids to the countryside.' When they talked about those dark days there was often a note of shame in their voices, as if they felt humiliated by the memory of their vulnerability. Even alpha-Sid spoke in a grim tone: 'That was scary, mate. I mean, not film scary. Really scary.'

As an outsider in 2008, it had looked like a genuinely serious crisis, but not end-of-the-world serious. The images that have come to define that episode — defeated-looking Lehman employees carrying cartons of their belongings through Wall Street — convey a certain lightness. As if it were only a matter of a few hundred overpaid people losing their jobs: *look at the Masters of the Universe now, brought down to our level*. It turns out, however, that those carton-carrying bankers were the beginning of what could very well have been an unimaginable catastrophe. I mean this literally, in the sense that financial experts do not seem to know what exactly could have happened except that it would have been beyond our wildest nightmares. They draw analogies to the financial equivalent of a nuclear meltdown, or to Armageddon, the biblical end time. In *Masters of Nothing: How the Crash Will Happen Again Unless We Understand Human Nature*, former economist at the Bank of England, Matthew Hancock, and pollster Nadhim Zahawi — now both members of parliament for the Conservatives — report that bankers were actually stocking up on guns, 'ready to bed down in bunkers if civil society collapsed.'

What was everyone so afraid of? In his book *The Origin of Financial Crises*, British fund manager George Cooper explains it like a simple domino effect: the collapse of one major bank could cause the global financial system to come to a halt, seize up and implode. Not only would this mean that we can no longer withdraw our money from banks but also that trade finance stops. As Cooper puts it, 'This financial crisis came perilously close to causing a systemic failure of the global financial system. Had this occurred, global trade would have ceased to function within a very short period of time. Remember that this is the age of just-in-time inventory management,' Cooper adds, meaning supermarkets have very small stocks. With impeccable understatement, Cooper concludes: 'It is sobering to contemplate the consequences of interrupting food supplies to the world's major cities for even a few days.'

These were the dominos that had come so close to falling down in 2008, and I had just witnessed first-hand what could be the next tile in that line. The summer of 2011 saw massive riots across London. These lasted only a few days and had nothing to do with the banks but the mechanism was there for all to see: no more than a few thousand people need go out plundering and the police are essentially powerless. Now imagine that hundreds of millions of people worldwide all hear at the same time that supplies have stopped to their supermarkets, pharmacies and petrol stations.

•

Al-Qaida utterly failed to break down life as we know it in the September 11 attacks on the World Trade Center in 2001, but the financial sector itself almost achieved it about seven years later. Now I saw what the next question was: can this happen again?

Step one had to be getting a grip on the finer detail of the sector. Where were the people who caused this? Fortunately, the layout of the financial world is not difficult to grasp. So let's imagine what a map of Planet Finance would look like.

Firstly you would see three enormous and contiguous continents: asset management, banking and insurance. Thanks to its sheer size, the last of that trio catches the eye first. Not only are hundreds of millions of lives, cars and holidays insured, but also ships, coal power plants, footballers' legs and financial products.

Insurance partly overlaps with banking, the second huge area of finance. The biggest players here are so-called commercial or retail banks. They offer insurance products – hence the overlap – but generate most of their revenues from activities that our grandparents would still recognise: the payment systems, savings accounts, mortgages and loans to small and medium-sized companies as well as major corporations and institutions. 'Commercial' is where the project finance banker works who loved driving through the country thinking, 'That is my toll bridge.'

As my interviewees pointed out, commercial banks are fundamentally different beasts to investment banks. In the latter, you'll see the traders on their trading floors, the dealmakers who get companies listed on the Stock Exchange, those who work in corporate finance or mergers and acquisitions, and also the 'structurers' who invent and build financial products – for instance the collateralised debt obligations (CDOs) we heard so much about thanks to the crash. Lehman Brothers was a 'pure' investment bank and Goldman Sachs still is; you cannot open a savings account with Goldman Sachs. There are purely commercial banks, and banks that are active in both areas, known as 'megabanks'; Bank of America, Citigroup, Deutsche Bank, BNP Paribas, Société Générale, HSBC and Barclays cater to customers who want a current account as well as entrepreneurs looking to get their company listed ('have it taken public'). The internal accountant who omitted her job from her online dating profile was working for a megabank, and had to get 'the numbers' both from investment and commercial bankers.

These are broad strokes, obviously, and zooming in you would find firms operating in the same markets without being a bank: mortgage providers compete with commercial banks, so-called boutique firms are in the same business as mergers and acquisitions dealmakers and brokers offer services also provided by trading floors in investment banks. Sid worked at one such brokerage firm, as was the interdealer broker who made the point that only a few per cent in the City make 'the huge sums.'

Most people who do enjoy huge sums of money need someone to invest it for them, which brings us to the third and last vast continent: asset management. These firms charge a fee for investing the money entrusted to them not only by wealthy people ('high net worth individuals'), but also from pension funds, rich oil countries and insurance companies, who have to put their premiums somewhere. There are plain asset managers who tend to invest in relatively straightforward bonds and shares. In addition, there are private equity firms that use their investors' capital to take over companies in order to sell them at a profit later on; hedge funds that follow 'unorthodox' investment strategies with high risks and rewards; while venture capitalists employ their expertise and clients' capital to help promising small companies and entrepreneurs grow. Nothing is ever simple in finance and there are overlaps here, too, when banks offer asset management services. The head of marketing who chose a career in the City because she had to raise a child on her own worked at her bank's asset management division.

Insurance, asset management and banking dominate

Planet Finance, but there are lots of islands scattered around them, providing services. Accountancy firms audit the books of companies and institutions, while credit ratings agencies classify the financial health of countries, companies and financial products – from 'junk-status' to signify that something is extremely risky to the widely known 'AAA' for super safe. There are the financial law and consultancy firms, the recruitment firms known as 'executive search,' financial IT companies, data management services in mergers and acquisitions and so on. As we zoom out we can also see the central bank and the regulators circling Planet Finance like satellites, trying to make sure from afar that everything is going according to the rules.

And now for the crash and the people who caused it. Since 2008, dozens of parliamentary commissions across the West have listened to witness testimonies and hundreds of reconstructions have been written by scientists and academics – in English alone the count is well past 300. This somewhat daunting tally of books would put off even the most dedicated of researchers. Fortunately, we now have a broad consensus about what happened – though not about who is ultimately to blame.

The short version is that in the years before the crash, commercial banks and mortgage providers lent far too much money to people who could not afford such debts primarily in the United States and the UK, mostly for mortgages. This continued over a long period of time because the easy money drove up house prices, making many people feel richer than they were. Also, commercial banks and mortgage providers had less reason to worry about the risk of default on these loans because they could sell them on to investment banks, which then chopped them up and repackaged them into ever more complex financial products. Asset managers at pension funds and other investors were keen to buy them because central banks were keeping interest rates low and these new instruments offered better returns. For protection, pension funds and others relied on the American insurance giant AIG, which insured many of the products. In turn, AIG trusted the credit rating agencies' triple-A ratings.

As time went on, the products became more and more intricate and 'exotic' but the triple-A ratings kept coming. Meanwhile, the banks kept some of these complex products on their own balance sheets – often hidden in deliberately complicated 'vehicles' in offshore tax havens. The accountants either failed to see any of this, or thought it was fine, or looked the other way, as did regulators and politicians.

In 2007, the Labour prime minister, Gordon Brown, praised a gathering of bankers and asset managers in a speech at Mansion House: 'The financial services sector in Britain, and the City of London at the centre of it, is a great example of a highly skilled, high value-added, talent-driven industry that shows how we can excel in a world of global competition. Britain needs more of the vigour, ingenuity and aspiration that you already demonstrate that is the hallmark of your success.'

At the time of that statement there were already signs that millions of house buyers would not be able to meet their financial obligations, particularly in the United States. The financial products that contained their mortgages began to lose value, or 'exploded' and became worthless. Investors had to take big losses but banks, too, had kept some of these products. They had to write off huge sums of money as well – but how much? Not only had many of the products themselves become mind-bogglingly difficult to value or understand but the same was also true of the 'vehicles' in offshore tax havens where the banks had placed many of them. Would the banks' buffers be big enough? At Lehman Brothers they were not, and when this bank had to announce bankruptcy other banks and financial institutions stopped lending each other money. Suddenly the financial world was gripped by a paralysing fear: what would happen tomorrow? Who would be the next to go belly up? The domino effect could cause the global financial system to collapse in a matter of days. In response, governments reached deep into the state coffers and central banks not only lowered interest rates to levels not seen in centuries but also pumped unprecedented amounts of newly created money into the economy, both directly and indirectly. This calmed the potentially debilitating distrust that had engulfed the financial system. Politicians and central bankers posed as fearless financial firemen – they had 'saved' the system.

Obviously there is more to a debacle as epic as the 2008 financial crisis and bail-out but even this crash course is enough to bring out the number of parties involved: the consumers who borrowed far beyond their means, often by misrepresenting or lying about their finances; the mortgage providers who encouraged people to borrow and cheat, or misled borrowers about the true extent of their indebtedness; the credit-rating agencies and accountancy firms that went along with the mushrooming complexity of products; the financial giant AIG which had insured them without keeping sufficient capital reserves. And how about the pension funds and other investors that had been clamouring for more complex financial instruments to buy, since these promised a good return and they were only allowed to invest in AAA products?

The list of parties to blame is in fact considerably longer yet two things already stand out. First, 'the bankers' were clearly not the only ones responsible. Second, most people working in the banks, as well as entire areas of 'finance,' had absolutely nothing to do with all of this.

Most commercial bankers were filling their days operating the payment system, or financing the construction of an oil rig, or dreaming up a new type of savings account for children under the age of twelve. The vast majority of accountants were at work auditing the books of energy companies, technology firms or government institutions, while the overwhelming majority of credit raters were studying the financial health of countries or corporations, far removed from financial products. Anyone involved in the stock market was miles removed from the 2008 debacle. The same goes for those who were busy taking companies public in, say, the Middle East or South America. And so on, until you get to the sales manager for mergers and acquisitions data services who enjoyed his foie gras in that restaurant at Covent Garden.

•

I remember a sense of relief, almost, when I began to understand just how few people were directly involved in the crash. At least this had not been a comprehensive conspiracy on the part of the entire sector. Indeed, the financial sector PR machine insists for good reason that almost nobody had seen a disaster of this magnitude coming. Not politicians, nor regulators, nor top economists at elite universities. Let's be reasonable, financial PR lobbyists would continue their argument: why would any banker deliberately run his bank into the ground? The crash of 2008 was a perfect storm, or rather a *black swan*: unique and literally unforeseeable. Since then the exploded products have been stripped of their risky elements, a mountain of extra rules and security measures have been implemented, while banks are working around the clock on cultural change. So . . . isn't the time for 'banker-bashing' over?

A perfectly styled top banker or PR operative can make this argument sound quite convincing. Until you turn it on its head. If you think about it, isn't it all the more alarming if virtually nobody in the sector realised how dangerous these complex financial products could be? The more I heard people declare that really, they had had no idea, the more I felt like someone who has woken from a nap on a bus only to be told by the driver that he has just managed to avoid plunging into a chasm that had suddenly opened up in the road. What an awful thing to hear, sitting at the back, ignorant and helpless. A feeling made worse when the driver adds: 'Well, sorry, but hey, nobody knew that this hole would open up here . . .'

Because then you begin to wonder: what other chasms are you unaware of?

It was plain to see that investment banks and investment divisions of megabanks had played a key role in the crash. And it was also clear that this was not the first time that investment bankers had had to say 'sorry' and promise to do better. During what came to be known as the dot-com bubble of the late nineties, investment bankers had praised and hyped worthless technology companies to investors and the financial media, while their colleagues in dealmaking were taking these companies public for eye-wateringly lucrative fees. When this internet bubble burst around the turn of the century an estimated $4,000 billion went up in smoke. To cushion this blow, central banks had lowered interest rates, creating lots of cheap money – which in turn contributed to the housing bubble that followed.

So, I decided to start digging into those investment banks.

3

Going Native

Now that I had a grip on the sector and the causes of the crash, my 'ignorance phase' had come to an end. I was about to become submerged in what psychologists call the 'denial stage.' The financial sector seems to be sending to send the same subliminal message: please go to sleep now, everything is safely back under control. And nobody does this as well as investment banks.

I managed to gain entry to the offices of a global investment bank only a handful of times. It is like stepping into an alien spaceship. The central lobby is as clean and shiny as a five-star hotel bathroom. Silent and incredibly fast lifts transport employees up to the sleek offices above, superbly confident security officers keep watch and polite desk-personnel efficiently go about their duties. The thick glass exterior blocks out all sounds from outside. The marble interior exudes cold power. The views from the highest floors make you feel literally on top of the world and on your way up there every banker you pass or meet in the lift routinely avoids eye contact; they seem full of purpose and restrained haste, absorbed in something immensely important. *We know what we are doing here so who are you to question us?*

I remember the first time I went to interview a vice president at an investment bank. I had sought out my best suit and least crumpled tie for the occasion. The banker in question was barely 30 years old! This is how job titles work in investment banks: 22-year-old university graduates start out modestly with the rank of analyst and then associate, but those who stay on become vice-president by the time they are 30 or so. Three or four years later your business card says director or senior vice-president, followed by the rank of managing director (MD). It is only those above the level of MD who are truly managing the bank: first the heads of a particular activity or region and above them the *cees* – people whose titles start with 'chief.' The chief of chiefs is the chief executive officer or CEO.

That is the pyramid and sometimes investment banks pay a price for giving so many people in their organisation an important-sounding job title. In the spring of 2012 one Greg Smith wrote a piece on *The New York Times* op-ed pages titled: 'Why I Am Leaving Goldman Sachs.' Smith was an executive director – that is what Goldman Sachs calls its vice-presidents. Columnists across the world gloated: a top banker had opened up about abuse and contempt for clients. What Smith revealed was certainly shocking (more of that later). But Smith was not a top banker. Goldman Sachs has thousands of 'executive directors.'

It took months to get a good sense of the architecture and culture of investment banks, and what surprised me was how unhelpful economists were – the very body of experts you'd think would be able to shed light on the world of high finance. However, economists do not carry out 'fieldwork.' An anthropologist who seeks to understand a group of people learns their language and moves into their community to spend months, if not years, systematically observing them. Economists have different methods, as the former director of the London School of Economics Howard Davies admits almost casually in his book, *The Financial Crisis: Who Is to Blame?* 'There is a lack of real-life research on trading floors themselves.'

To get some idea of the daily routine in investment bankers in London, I started out by reading anonymous blogs written by bankers whose authenticity and credibility was difficult to assess. I studied memoirs published by former City employees. A post-crash genre of books had sprung up with titles promising drugs, sex and extravagantly bad behaviour: *Binge Trading: The Real Inside Story of Cash, Cocaine and Corruption in the City*; *Gross Misconduct: My Year of Excess in the City*; *Confessions of a City Girl: The Devil Wears Pinstripes*. Barbara Stcherbatcheff's story starts in a strip club, which also occupies significant sections of Tetsuya Ishikawa's *How I Caused the Credit Crunch: A Vivid and Personal Account of Banking Excess*. The best known of those books is *Cityboy: Beer and Loathing in the Square Mile* by Geraint Anderson. In this semi-fictional autobiography, he spends 200 pages drinking, snorting coke, ogling strippers, chasing whores and, above all, complaining about hangovers. It is an entertaining read. It was also immensely lucrative for its author – according to Anderson, *City Boy* has sold a quarter of a million copies. However, the contrast between these books and the investment bankers I met could not have been starker.

Why not start with the very first investment banker to agree to an interview? An inconspicuously well-dressed deal-maker in his early forties with the rank of managing director, he had included the time zone ('1 p.m. UK') when setting up our appointment because just that morning he had returned from a business trip to New York. For a good 15 years now he had been working in mergers and acquisitions, which meant that he was a kind of financial contractor co-ordinating the sale or purchase of companies or parts of companies on behalf of his clients, all of whom were major global corporations. I asked how that translates into an average working day and his answer came down to one word: meetings. Meetings with potential buyers of companies, meetings with sellers of companies, meetings with buyers or sellers of parts of companies, as well as meetings with the army of lawyers, accountants and financial services providers that surround any major deal. And of course with colleagues: 'As an MD you are entitled to have lunch in the executive dining room with other managing directors. This is an excellent informal setting to catch up on recent developments and future trends with the other leaders of our firm.' The rest of his time he was flying across the world to keep up with his clients or he might invite them over to London, for a day at Wimbledon, for example. 'We may talk about business. But it's still a very pleasant place to be.'

This is how it works, he explained. You have your own region with a number of corporations in it. You advise them on strategy and developments in their sector, year in year out, all unpaid. However, should one of 'your' corporations decide on a major financial transaction you expect to do that deal for them, and be paid a good fee. Hence the bonus system. In years without deals there is no income, so the bank pays a relatively modest base salary. In good years there is a lot coming in and therefore a lot to be shared around.

Was it true that in a good year an MD like him could expect to make over a million pounds? He gave me a smile. 'Money is important, but more as a marker, an acknowledgment. I am not a flashy guy and my car is 11 years old. A bonus means somebody has taken notice that you have done a good job.' Outsiders have funny ideas about bankers, he said. 'Most people on my level lead balanced lives with families and kids. Our firm provides health checks, subsidised gym access and lectures on food and sleeping patterns, on how to deal with stress and the whole kids, family, nannies thing.'

This is a high adrenaline job, he agreed, which was one reason he enjoyed it so much: 'In negotiations you wear each other out first, and only at the very last moment you make concessions. So most negotiations go on for a long time and are concluded in the evening, at night or on weekends.'

I asked about taboos, and suggested in a clumsy attempt to break the ice that presumably bankrupting the bank would be a big one? Without hesitation or a smile, he said, 'No: breaching confidentiality and dishonesty. I am negotiating on a client's behalf. If your integrity is in doubt, forget it.' Clients expect outstanding financial analysis and advice so attention to detail is very important, he went on, and a lot comes down to judgment. 'One client tells me about their plans for the Indian market. How much of that can I share with another client, for whom that information could be very valuable?'

But the disastrous risks that banks take, what did he have to say about that? He cleared his throat, in what looked like mild embarrassment: 'I don't lend or borrow any money. I am a financial advisor. I cannot generate losses, worst comes to the worst I don't make the bank any money. The real damage I can do is in the field of reputation, by bringing the bank into disrepute. Around here that would be the ultimate taboo.'

The bankers I was speaking to appeared to be so normal, so human. They talked intelligently and seemed far from the monsters I'd read about. It took me a long time – maybe a few months – to get beyond this version of reality and to get a grip on what a deeply dysfunctional place the City is.

Consider the 'rock-'n'-roll trader.' He was a little over 30 years old and had been with a prestigious investment bank for around 10 years, buying and selling financial products on behalf of clients. His rank was now director: 'Trading is binary at its core, black and white. I have generated value today, or I

haven't. Then there is the glamour of it. You know – the money,
the girls, rock 'n' roll without the guitars. In trading you get to
define yourself from an early age,' he said. 'You come in at 22
and you can prove yourself right away. I know guys making £1
million a year at 25. Not a lot, but it does happen and that's
such a contrast with other jobs.'

It was the early evening and we were meeting in Lombard
One, a restaurant near Bank tube station that is popular with
City workers and where a beer goes for four pounds. The trader
grew up in a poor Asian immigrant family but thanks to his
gift for maths he got scholarships for an exclusive private school
and then a top university. Most of his primary-school friends
were unemployed or working low-end jobs like security – and
if you put all of their income together it was probably less than
he made on his own. 'If you don't come from money,' he said in
a matter-of-fact tone, 'you realise early on that actually, money
is quite important.'

I brought up the crash and he shook his head: 'There seems
to be this blanket anger towards bankers. Going over the comments on your blog it struck me that people seem to think all of
us saw the crisis coming. But apart from Goldman and maybe
Deutsche Bank, nobody expected this.' By which he did not
mean *everybody* at Goldman Sachs or Deutsche Bank. 'I am
also angry about the crisis. When I think of the CEO of some
Wall Street bank that went bust, and he still has his $400 mil-
lion . . . I mean, I owned shares in some of these banks, and
they've gone to zero.'

It's like suggesting that all sportspeople are bad because of
one doping scandal or obnoxious misconduct by a single footballer. But even among traders, there are huge differences, he
went on, depending on whether you are trading shares, commodities such as oil, coffee or grain, foreign currencies, bonds,
interest rates instruments or the more complex products.

Even traders in shares – 'equity' for insiders – must be sub-divided, he went on. Some trade shares in the oil and gas sector, others in telecoms, or in financial companies.

That is quite a lot to digest for outsiders, I suggested, but he was not done. 'You've got prop traders who use the bank's money to make money for the bank. And flow traders, like me, who trade on behalf of clients. Again, a huge difference.' For flow, the Holy Grail is to become prop, he said, and be away from all the politics, salespeople, clients. Prop is the purest form of trading, he thought, and he was very sorry to see it dying out because regulators don't want banks to take risks with their own capital.

I ordered more beer. 'Another thing,' he said. 'Outsiders who think, "I could do this." When we hire people we tell them, you have to be comfortable with running an amount of risk every day of your working life. You end up thinking about it in your sleep, while you eat. It starts when you wake up and never goes away. On an emotional level, it's not that easy.'

Tell me about a day at the office, I said when the beers arrived.

'At the beginning of the day I have a "view" of how the market will go. On that basis I will take "positions" [binding commitments to buy or sell a given amount of financial instruments such as shares, bonds, currencies or commodities, for a given price]. Then I wait for clients to call, or be called by our salespeople [the middlemen], who want to buy some of that position. We pocket a commission for the transaction, and we may make money from the margin between what I bought the contracts for, and what I sold them on to clients for.'

That is of course the simplified version, he emphasised, just like his characterisation earlier of trading as beautifully black and white. 'Actually, there is grey. There's office politics involved when it gets decided what book you trade – for example, the oil and gas sector, or the financials sector. Clearly, there can be more client flow in one book than in another.'

There is jealousy on the trading floor, he said. 'Of course. People whispering, "He had a really easy book to trade," after you had a good year.' The low point is when everybody around you is making money and for some reason you are not, he continued. 'Everyone has bad periods, like sportspeople. You need to be strong, tell yourself, "It's fine, and I'm good." It's everyone's fear: to have lost it.'

But what is 'it'? 'Call it intuition, call it the equivalent of what Messi can do with a ball. In the morning you ask traders who have "it", what do you think the market is going to do? And they go: "up." And up it goes. It's quite something.'

Ruefully, he acknowledged that some consider traders as little more than gamblers. He took my notebook and filled up two pages with mathematical formulas and Greek letters, to explain the mathematics behind his work. We got talking about the trading floor and all of a sudden he was full of energy again: 'There you are, sitting with two levels of screens in front of you. You know that the guy to your right and the guy to your left both understand exactly what it is you're doing. We all have the same desire: to get on the floor, to make money.' Think of it as a playground, he said, grinning. 'Jokes can be about your weight, hair, the university you went to. It's an expression of camaraderie. I was in a minority in a white school and I have learnt to see how a comment about my background is meant.'

Now he looked genuinely happy and excited. 'I wish I could take you on the trading floor. There's no privacy, people are meant to overhear each other on the phone. The toilets are always in a horrible condition. I don't know why. Because people on a trading floor are animals? It's just how it is. I love to be one of those people there, the energy, and the buzz . . . It's almost like an opera.'

•

The more investment bankers I met the more I learnt to see this type of bank as consisting of a complicated cluster of islands that operate under one flag. The full job titles they introduced themselves with in their emails said it all: Managing Director, Equity Capital Markets Oil and Gas, North America; Mergers and Acquisitions, Telecom Europe Middle East Africa (Director); Vice-President, Equity Derivatives Structurer, Europe. At first these email signatures sounded like a secret language, but they are simply the co-ordinates people use to locate themselves in that enormous bank of theirs: rank, activity, sector, region. The traders in their respective niches, dealmakers in mergers and acquisitions, IPOs or corporate finance, the professional investors in asset management . . . When asked about their responsibility for the crash they could join all those others in the City in saying: 'It wasn't me.' That even applies to most of the 'structurers' who invent or build complex financial products. Investment banks have a vastly larger array of such products besides the ones that blew up in 2008. So huge have investment banks become that they can give rise to subcultures, and even subcultures within subcultures. There is trading, and within that flow trading, and within that commodities flow trading commodities. Each market comes with its own codes, vocabulary and rituals and its own set of buyers and sellers, internal dynamics and outside pressures. It matters whether you trade in wheat or pig bellies that will at some point be eaten, or in a 'safe' precious metal like silver. Weather plays no role in gold trading, as there is no such thing as a failed harvest in gold. The price of oil can help decide an election, something the price of coffee cannot do.

Consider the quants (short for quantitative analysts, these

are the people that design and implement the complex financial models that underpin the banking system). The quants seem to form a caste of their own, cutting across all ranks, job titles, activities and hierarchies. 'In some ways a quant at UBS will identify more with another quant at JP Morgan than with his non-quant colleague sitting next to him,' said a quant who had risen very high at his bank. Quants typically have PhDs in maths, or theoretical physics or chemistry, and many would describe themselves simply: 'I am a quant' – as if that was all I needed to know about them. They spoke of a 'brotherhood of the nerds' and sometimes behaved like priests who are alone in having access to the Holy Book and thereby to the secrets of the universe. Non-quants often talked about them in dismissive terms: 'You just need to get a few quants for that.'

If quants and non-quants seemed mostly to ignore each other, the antagonism between traders and dealmakers in mergers and acquisitions was palpable, as rivalrous as two local football teams. Initially the majority of volunteers for the blog were dealmakers. That was because of the type of people in trading, a senior dealmaker explained. 'Our kind is more likely to read a quality paper like the *Guardian*.' A trader I put this to burst out laughing: 'Dealmakers volunteer in droves because they have nothing to do. The economy is lying tits up! There are simply no mergers and acquisitions happening!'

Dealmakers described traders as 'street fighters' and in turn traders called dealmakers a 'pure waste of office space' who peddle 'reputation insurance.' 'Say you are a corporate CEO about to do a big merger or acquisition,' said a trader. 'You hire Goldman Sachs and everything goes wrong. Now, nobody is going to blame you for hiring the number one investment bank in the world. So you're safe.'

The rock-'n'-roll trader spoke with near-disgust of mergers and acquisitions, stating quite simply that he could never work there. 'You don't really get to do anything of value in the first years. Worst of all: you almost have to puff yourself up. Why would clients pay for your advice, unless you are the smartest person on earth? It's a salesman's job – you know, a dirty job.'

•

Anthropologists have taboos, too. On top of the list comes discrimination, immediately followed by its opposite: going native. You spend months in the jungle of Papua New Guinea and, over time, human sacrifice begins to look pretty reasonable. As a nod to this natural tendency to identify with the people you are investigating, the *Guardian* blog had been given the subtitle 'going native in the world of finance' and this proved prescient. Practically every interview on the blog with an investment banker was greeted in the comment thread below with terms like 'psychopath,' 'gambling addict' or 'parasite.' The third label particularly infuriated the investment bankers and as I listened to their arguments I could not help thinking: you have a point.

We are providing a service, they said, and those services must be useful to our clients or they would not buy them, would they? When interviewees were British they added that the financial sector contributes many billions in taxes to the treasury and creates hundreds of thousands of jobs both directly in the financial industry and indirectly in the restaurants, hotels, airports, conference centres and taxi firms that depend on the sector. What else can our country do, they would ask. Our manufacturing industry has vanished long ago. How would London fare without bankers? Do you think that all those world-class museums, parks and football clubs could exist without their sponsors in the financial sector?

Professional investors in asset management divisions would ask rhetorically: your readers are saving up for a pension, aren't they? Now, there are two wind turbine factories. Which one should your pension money be invested in? Somebody needs to work out which one is managed best and most deserving of new capital; that's us.

A merger or acquisition easily affects legal systems in five or six countries, dealmakers said. There are tax laws to deal with, environmental laws, labour laws, competition laws, pension laws . . . Getting that right takes real work. Trademakers, too, had their own defence. Somebody has to execute client's orders in the markets. How else is your pension fund to make investments?

And those who design and build complex financial products and instruments produced quite reasonable-sounding hypothetical scenarios that illustrated their work. One example: 'An African airliner is selling tickets for January next year. But if the oil price shoots up in December they are in trouble because they will have sold lots of tickets too cheaply. So they need to avoid paying more for oil in January than its current price. We build such an instrument and go looking for a party that needs to protect itself against a lower oil price in January. In the ideal scenario the two make a perfect match and we have helped two parties "hedge" against a risk. Our reward is a commission.'

Every division in investment banks had a story like this ready, and the work they did seemed to have very little to do with parasites or gambling. An average working day involved collecting, selecting, bartering, interpreting and passing on information and analyses, under time pressure and in competition with rivals at other banks or financial firms. Nothing too sinister there.

A corporate finance dealmaker with the rank of managing director explained that his job was playing middleman between multinationals and other big financial players looking for money to borrow, and the investors in his network looking for a place for their money. 'You must be able to make people feel comfortable enough to share information,' he went on. 'Negotiating skills are important, and an ability to weigh risk. I am dependent on other people's risk estimates and I have to be able to filter. When someone is screaming on the phone, is he really mad and with his back to the wall? Or is it a negotiating ploy?'

My job is a kind of game or daily puzzle, people said, sometimes to their surprise. Of course you need analytical intelligence and perseverance to play that game and solve the puzzle, but at least as important are social skills, trust and confidentiality.

'Peoplethinktheworldof finance is aboutcompetition,' said a former sales trader in her late twenties. 'Sure, there is that. But most of all it's about co-operation.' Traders need to concentrate on developments in the markets so they don't speak to clients; instead they leave this to the sales traders within their investment bank. Both sets of colleagues have to work together. She had worked in bonds (loans that can be traded) and her clients were big professional investors. I asked for an example of cooperation, preferably as basic as possible, and she took her time to think of one. 'Say a company in which my client holds corporate bonds goes bust – meaning in simplified terms that the defaulted company owes my client money. The corporate bonds are now "troubled" and my client wants to sell them. What is the right price?'

That will be determined in court, but those lawsuits take forever and her client wants to sell now. 'So our trader gives my client a price and the client asks me, why this price? It'll be my job to explain about the lawsuits here and there, the ins and outs of the case. What this means is I read and read and read.'

Which is where the co-operation and people skills come in. 'You can go through all the reading material yourself but it's much faster if you can call someone up and say, give me a 10-line summary of what's going on.' That is why it is vital that many people in the bank like you, she said, especially those over at the researchers' desk. It was difficult to see this sales trader as a parasite, gambling addict or monster. In fact, quite a few investment bankers talked about themselves and their bank with a clear sense of ironic detachment.

A sales trader in his late forties had been awarding bonuses to juniors for a number of years now. How did that work? He laughed out loud: 'Basically it's a bunch of guys in a room going over a list of names and accounts and saying, "OK, so how much do we give this guy?"'

The first year he was part of this bunch of guys he made a terrible mistake. 'I thought, I am going to fight for the people in my team to get what they deserve. Wrong. After I had settled on those numbers, senior management came in and cut all bonuses by 20 per cent. Headquarters took off another 15 per cent. The following year I added 40 per cent over what I thought reasonable and that's how it played out. By cutting bonuses senior management proves to headquarters they have the bank's interest at heart – while probably leaving more for the top. Headquarters must be seen by shareholders to be doing the same.'

The bonus culture is a ritual on many levels. 'The pre-positioning starts in September to October. People fly their kite, signalling to their boss: "Look how well I have done over the past year"; "Remember the account that went so well, I was on board." When a big deal is announced, people try to get their names mentioned. We call that "revenue tourism." Meanwhile management is pushing back: this year is not going to be the big one. The economy/our bank/department/desk . . . There is always one of them that hasn't done well and hence is a "drag." They are managing and talking down expectations.'

Then it is bonus or 'comp' (compensation) day. Nobody is allowed to reveal their bonus and in some banks it is a sackable offence to do so: grounds for immediate dismissal. At the same time people are told their 'number' in glass corner offices. Everybody gets to see the spectacle. 'The idea is that you explode,' the sales trader said drily. 'Many colleagues will try to make management think they should have got far, far more. You see colleagues smashing their fist on the table, with the manager keeping a poker face and probably saying, "You know it's enough."'

After an interview with somebody like this sales trader I often caught myself thinking: if we had been colleagues we could have become friends. This is not how anthropologists are meant to think. As if to increase the temptation to identify still more, some investment bankers had jobs almost identical to that of a journalist. For example I met a man who had been working as a research analyst at a major bank for over a decade – he was now a director. He followed a set of companies in a particular sector as closely as he could, to send his analyses and recommendations to big investors: buy, sell, hold or neutral. When the financial media report that 'analysts reacted with disappointment to such-and-such's results,' they are talking about his kind of people. Let me name this research analyst after the bonus he received last year: the million-dollar banker.

'My job is a lot like being a journalist,' he wrote in his email and when we meet in the early evening he added: 'When I hear hacks talk about their frustrations, it's usually that they lack resources to go deep, they don't get paid enough, their readership doesn't pay attention.' Compare that to me, he said with a grin. He got to follow seven or eight companies really thoroughly, while the 2,000 people or so who receive his analysis do tend to read it because they pay tens of thousands of pounds for it.

I got us another drink. He was a sturdy man, around 40

years old, who characterised his politics as 'pretty left-wing.' After a swig of his beer he pointed out that in the blog I was 'trying to get to the bottom of something to make it understandable for others. That is what research analysts do, too. Except you are writing for an audience that knows nothing about the subject whereas I am writing for people who are equally knowledgeable.'

I asked for an example and he emphasised that he would have to simplify a bit: 'Say you are a research analyst for the global steel sector and one day you receive a tip from someone who knows that you speak Italian: take a good look at the pension obligations of a corporation XYZ in Italy. So you go to Italy to spend weeks digging through the relevant laws. You talk to union people, legal experts, and the firm's management . . . Eventually you work out that thanks to some obscure rule the steel corporation has to pay out considerably less in pensions than assumed. You send a report to your clients who buy shares in that corporation. As the obscure rule becomes more widely known the share price goes up – the lower the pension liabilities, the higher the corporation's value. Your clients sell their shares and make a nice profit.'

Except for that last step this did sound a lot like investigative journalism. 'I will say it's an amazing pain to start your working day so early,' million-dollar banker concluded. 'But I love my job and I take care not to take it overly seriously. The work is very interesting, with a bit of the fruit-machine dynamic, the instant enforcement mechanism when the market validates something you said.'

•

The fact was, I had a lot in common with the investment bankers I was meeting. The City is an extraordinarily international place and an estimated 40 per cent of investment bankers were born outside the UK. So they were ex-pats like me. But the affinity went far deeper, with Brits and non-Brits alike: we had all had the same sort of university education and had spent quite a few years abroad, as a student or for work. We spoke other languages, loved the same kind of films, books and music, read the same newspapers and magazines, and went on the same kind of holidays.

In short, though they were making considerably more money than I did, we belonged to the same social-cultural class and as I got to know more colleagues in London it became clear that I was not alone in this. Many British journalists have a partner, family members or friends working in the City. Many journalists went to Oxford, Cambridge or the London School of Economics – the same recruiting grounds of investment banks.

I could go native, concluding that investment banks have indeed cleaned up their act. We still need real action on bonuses but apart from that . . . Investment bankers themselves seem decent enough people, so why would their organisation not be decent enough, too? Idiots are everywhere so it stands to reason that in such vast organisations every now and again something goes wrong and an incident happens. As for the crash, well, how many people predicted the tsunami in Fukushima?

Fortunately the blogs with investment bankers triggered reactions from unexpected corners. And those interviewees told very different stories indeed.

4

Other People's Money

When interviewing the first batch of investment bankers I did not really know what to look for. Their banks were more than a riddle where you seek an answer to a question. They were a mystery: what was the question and who to put it to? Interviewees were not going to sit down with me to explain how the City was laying the ground for a new crash or the next scandal. Such individuals – if they even existed – would not agree to an interview in the first place, let alone volunteer for one.

Nevertheless, emails began to arrive from people working in the back office and the middle office of investment banks. When investment bankers wrote in to volunteer for an interview they were often brimming with self-confidence, particularly the men, and many presented their offer as a favour: 'I find your project interesting. If you can guarantee my anonymity I am prepared to meet.' With back- and middle-office employees the tone was rather different: 'You are probably very busy concentrating on real bankers. But should you want to hear the story of someone in a role like mine, I can do most evenings.'

A man who had spent the past five years in support functions on a trading floor wrote: 'Your readers so far have been fed on a constant diet of traders and mergers and acquisitions bankers. These guys represent no more than 5 per cent of the finance community but receive 90 per cent of the publicity. The other downtrodden 95 per cent need some representation too.'

A second difference emerged when we met. Back- and middle-office staff get paid far less so they cannot afford expensive clothes, watches, phones or pens. Nor are they 'client-facing,' meaning they do not get to see clients and need not impress anyone with their appearance.

In a restaurant close to her bank at Canary Wharf I had lunch with an IT worker. She had short hair and was wearing the typical uniform of someone in a support function: informal but smart. As she ordered a vegetarian pizza and a glass of tap water it was clear she was nervous: what if a colleague saw her? She remembered all too well how a silence had fallen at the family table after she announced her new job. Her sister had accused her of being 'one of the bankers now.' The thing is, she said, the kind of work she does isn't specific to finance. At the time she was working on a trading floor to automate data input processes – replacing manual tasks with computers. 'In one way I am putting people out of work,' she shrugged. 'There's a constant drive at banks to do that. There is reorganisation all the time and every time a new boss comes in, she needs to show she can cut costs.'

The traders loved making fun of her working-class northern accent. She called them 'posh' in return. It's all pretty good-humoured, she said, 'but a different world all the same, theirs and mine.' The other day a banker had turned to her. He had just worked out that after school fees, mortgage payments etc, he was left with only the minimum wage to spend. She had asked him, what did he think ordinary people on a minimum wage lived on, after they paid all their bills? 'He was really confused, and admitted that he had never actually realised that for ordinary people everything has to come out of the minimum wage, that it's not free money to spend on whatever you like.'

She paused. 'I sit next to this girl who has a son whom she never sees. She gets in very early, goes out very late, and the nanny sits at home. Money can never be a subsitute for love, I don't think.'

She was making close to £80,000 a year, plus a bonus of around 10 per cent – in good years. She'd never tell friends back home about that. 'I really feel a bit fraudulent,' she said quietly, 'doing this job that isn't that special.' It would be paid much less if it weren't based in London. 'Rents here are insane.' She preferred to commute even though it's three hours in the morning and three hours in the evening, every day. 'I get a lot of reading done.' Her husband had what she called 'a straight-forward manual job.' The two of them had never scaled up their lives, she said, and they were saving whatever they did not need. 'This means I can quit this job whenever I want and go back to the life I had, have kids and actually see them grow up. I am still free.'

Another back-office employee I met worked as a chief operating officer in a megabank. Her job was to manage the operations of a 400-people-strong trading floor – all of them trading in equities, i.e. shares. She described her job as 'making it easier for our people to make money for the bank,' perhaps by streamlining some part of the organisation. Asked about the best moments for her, she said: 'When somebody at a desk cries out: "Yes, this makes my life easier."' Given all the jargon she had found it impossible to explain to her parents what she was doing, let alone how much she enjoyed her job. When her children were younger they thought she was a teller, 'one of those people in a polyester jacket. For them that was what someone who works in a bank looks like.'

In this kind of job you cannot be good on your first day,

she explained. 'You need to learn who is lying to you, what's happened in the past and when people have made mistakes. For that you need their respect, so they tell you that a mistake has been made. Respect is something you earn over time – you can't have it handed over to you by your predecessor.'

Twenty years ago while travelling abroad she got a job at a bank, 'really at the lowest level imaginable.' She had worked her way up and by now she was 'something in the vicinity of £200,000 plus bonuses, which vary from year to year but on average fall somewhere between £50,000–£150,000.' In a bad year her bonus could also be zero, she stressed.

This was a different world to the one I'd previously encountered. If one were drawing a diagram, an investment bank would be divided into three layers or castes. On top is the relatively small group of people who get all the attention and big bonuses: the front office. These are the actual bankers. Helping them is a huge support apparatus on the bottom layer that ranges from legal to internal accounting, IT services to human resources, PR and communication to the graphics department, the latter available 24/7, and of course the whole bureaucracy surrounding a trade – the people who arrange transfers to and from clients and who report to internal and external accountants and to the regulators.

All these support functions are known as the back office, which leaves the layer in between: the middle office, or 'risk and compliance.' These are the people responsible for internal controls. Compliance is there to make sure everything goes according to the book. Risk managers monitor the gambles that investment bankers take or are proposing to take, saying no to overly reckless plans and pressing 'stop' when activities get out of hand. The number of rules that banks have to comply with is huge, and therefore so are the compliance departments. Risk departments are a varied bunch – some people specialise in the odds that the individual, company or government the bank is dealing with may get into financial difficulties. Others look at what might happen to the loan, trade or deal their bank is considering or involved in should the markets suddenly go down. There is also 'operational risk': how do we prevent our infrastructure from crashing or being abused? And 'sovereign risk': what are the chances of instability in the country our bank is dealing with?

'I remember at times feeling immense relief in looking at the calendar and realising that a particular loan would be paid back on that day, thinking: "Thank God",' a sovereign risk manager told me. It meant his bank no longer ran a risk on that loan. He had just retired, or rather, just been fired. But with a 'reasonable settlement' so he had no complaints.

The more precarious a country is judged to be by people like him, the harder it becomes for investment bankers to do a deal or trade there. 'You might say the stereotypes sit at the two ends of the spectrum for human emotions – aggression for traders and dealmakers, a certain degree of paranoia for risk and compliance people.' Bankers hoping to do deals with a country naturally try to lower our risk estimates, he said. 'That is why you need strong people in risk and compliance.'

Was the middle office strong enough to resist this pressure? Well, he answered evasively, 'a lot has changed since the 1970s. Overall finance has become much more meritocratic and diverse. On the negative side, the sector as a whole has become relentlessly focused on profit, and out to screw the customer. Much of banking is best done as a public utility. Let's say I'm not a fan of financial deregulation.'

I asked about the crash and he explained with a distinct sense of pride that his team had seen the implosion of the American housing market coming. 'What we didn't catch was just how awful it would be.' They had assumed that, thanks to the new generation of complex financial products, risks had been spread over so many points that the system as a whole was stable. He remembered, 'as if it were yesterday,' sitting in his office with his colleagues in 2008 and seeing another institution's share price collapse. They would sing 'Another One Bites the Dust' together. 'It was frightening to be there and see it unravel. The global economy came very close to seizing up. You'd resort to gallows hamour to deal with it.'

They were truly different beasts in the back and middle office. In interviews I sometimes used a lateral question to get people to talk about their jobs in a different way: what animal would you be? A compliance officer replied: 'Animal? I am the zoo-keeper!' Another compliance officer compared himself to a 'dog who likes to be kicked. We work on behalf of management, we are loyal, we go fetch their sticks. We bark at people when they do the wrong thing. We get some things wrong ourselves, we get kicked and then we do it again.'

A product controller who had to check and verify the profit and loss accounts for traders said: 'What sort of animal goes around lots of other animals but doesn't get eaten? Also, there's lots of us, and we are engaged in an activity that in and of itself makes no sense but which is indispensable in the greater scheme of things. Maybe bees? Or ants?'

An internal accountant first thought of a springbok: 'Pretty mundane, operate in groups, quite nice.' Internal accountants are a bit slower though, she continued. They are the sort of people who try do do things properly, who fear getting it wrong. They are industrious. 'Maybe beavers?' Someone who had worked in human resources at a big bank for many years said that people like him 'exist to help others excel. Is there an animal that lets another animal do that? If the alpha male chimpanzee is the leader of the pack, I would say we are beta male chimpanzees: there to make others achieve their goals.'

That is how people in the back and middle offices thought of themselves. Now the front office. 'Let me see,' a sales trader in complex financial products said. 'We work in groups and we go out and hunt for clients. We share the spoils . . . Wolves, maybe?'

'We are tigers,' said another flow trader. 'You want traders to be as aggressive as they can and make the bank as much money as possible.' The 'risk limits' that he had to stay in were his cage.

A third trader described his own kind as hyenas and the structurers who design and build complex financial products as velociraptors. When I put this to one such structurer he said he saw traders as baboons: 'Can be aggressive but nice most of the time.' The markets are a shark tank, he went on, while structurers like him were not carnivorous prehistoric reptiles but rather creatures that patiently wait their chance to strike: 'Snakes.'

The only two groups in the front office not to choose a predator to describe themselves were quants, such as one wizard I spoke to who had built a mathematical model to exploit tiny, temporary price differences between financial markets ahead of everyone else: 'We are the birds that live on a hippopotamus. We find our meal in between the hippo's teeth, in other words: we make the market more efficient. The hippo tolerates us.'

The others were investment bankers in asset management whose job it is to invest money on behalf of rich clients and big financial institutions, for a fixed fee – perhaps not by coincidence one of the most tightly regulated areas. 'We are tortoises,' said one such banker with the rank of managing director. 'We are not hunters and have a long life because we are careful.' It's a tough world out there, she said with a resigned smile, so bankers in asset management develop a hard shell. 'We can be the butt of jokes for what others perceive as our slowness. In reality we are deliberate; if necessary we can move surprisingly fast. We are not herd animals. But we are quite happy to spend time in the vicinity of our fellows.'

•

We are so used to hearing politicians and columnists deride investment banks as 'casinos' or the Wild West that it comes almost as a surprise to be reminded that these banks have thousands of people whose job it is to prevent scandals and crashes. Now the obvious question was: middle office in risk and compliance, why aren't you doing your job?

The code of silence was going to make it very difficult to arrange interviews with middle-office employees who had given the green light to the toxic financial products that became world-famous in 2008. But the crash was not the only time that risk and compliance must have failed. Around the turn of the century, investment banks were mired in the dot-com bubble and, in the years to follow, scandal after scandal broke. Traders at a range of investment and megabanks were found to have manipulated crucial interest rates and foreign currency rates, resulting in the Libor and FX affairs. In spite of all the internal controls and risk limits, another rogue trader at the London headquarters of the Swiss bank UBS managed to lose his bank billions of pounds. The megabank HSBC was caught laundering drugs money while several banks were fined for busting sanctions against Iran and Sudan. In 2012, a trader known as the London Whale lost over $6 billion at JP Morgan. And for years now across Europe, small and medium-sized companies, pension funds, utilities, municipalities and other public institutions have been discovering that the complex financial products they bought from London-based investment bankers have turned 'toxic.' The list of scandals gets longer with every passing year, and who knows what else has been kept under wraps?

Investment banks and the financial lobby try to portray each disaster as the work of a few rotten apples, much like they had characterised the crash as a one-off accident. What did the middle office think?

By way of explanation, one compliance officer at a major bank gave me an insight into how the front-office dealmakers view the middle office, the very people who are meant to be holding the reins and overseeing them in order to prevent these scandals occurring. 'In my first week in this job, I was sitting outside with some people from the bank, having a beer and telling a joke,' she said. 'They were completely surprised. They said: "Aren't you in risk and compliance?" I said I was. They went: "But one, you're drinking, two, you were telling a joke, and three, you appear to have a personality."' Bankers look at the compliance department the way footballers look at linesmen, she continued. 'Losers running back and forth along a line, stopping players from scoring or doing great things.'

It was the same for the back-office staff. A man who had worked for a number of years in a support role at a bank until he was made redundant a few months earlier described the power balance thus: 'Back-office people are always enormously intimidated by the traders. You know which ones have a huge P and L and are making a lot for the bank. Their reputation precedes them. Most have nicknames. Hotshot traders can be abrupt and abrasive, always under pressure. You learn to pick you moments for a query.'

You could tell when back-office employees needed to get in touch with traders, he continued. They would be taking an unusually long time crafting an email, hesitating to pick up the phone.

'Nobody ever challenges the front office,' said another compliance officer with over a decade of experience on several trading floors at major banks. 'I've never seen it happen.'

A recently retired risk manager remembered how the men on the trading floor would sometimes go to play football after work. 'One time we were late, so we took taxis. The traders could claim that through expenses without a second thought, but we couldn't. It was only a few pounds, obviously, so it was all about the symbolism. We refused to pay, causing a huge headache for various managers who blamed each other for the petty rule. This went on for weeks before we paid up.'

You can see our lower status by our nicknames, said middle-office workers. Investment bankers are rock stars, rainmakers, the dark side, movers and shakers or big swinging dicks. Meanwhile we are the business blockers, deal killers, show stoppers, box tickers and cost centres.

People talked about Bic pens for them and expensive fountain pens for the front office, and how those in the back and middle office who were hoping to be promoted would buy the luxury pens to signal their ambition. Because that could happen: a trader or banker asks someone in support or internal controls to come work for them in the front office.

A woman in a support function explained that she always dressed in a subdued, conservative way. No nail polish. Trouser suits not a skirt. 'If you look at the trading floor today,' she said, 'there are quite a few women working there, in support functions, whose goal it seems is to hook a trader. Can't get a footballer, so get a trader, you know. Sometimes when I see the way they dress – short skirt, boobs out – I ask myself: are we on a beach?'

I didn't ever hear anyone say: 'Oh yes, the front office is trembling before us.' Nor did an investment banker ever speak with respect about the middle office. Sometimes the tone was neutral, for instance this from the rock-'n'-roll trader: 'We seem to be seen as gamblers, but I know of few people who live up to that cliché. It's really quite hard to take a huge gamble. There's risk and compliance; you have risk limits you can't exceed. If you suddenly take a massive position, somebody will see it.'

But usually the front office reserved the same term for 'internal controls' they used for regulators: losers.

Everybody stressed that investment banks do their utmost to be compliant, and every step or move has to be signed off by a vast bureaucracy. But all this is seen as 'box-ticking,' they would go on, and just because in theory the middle office has the power to stop wrongdoing, it does not mean that they can do so in practice.

Some believed that their powerlessness was simply embedded in investment banks' DNA. First, it is very difficult to put a number on a loss you have averted by saying no, people argued. By contrast, when a deal goes through, the trader or dealmaker can point to the profits made for the bank. More important still: the front office earns the revenues out of which the middle-office salaries are paid. This automatically lower the latter's status.

That sounded convincing but there is a deeper explanation. Pick up any financial history book and all the middle-office lamenting falls into place. Yes, the salaries of those who manage the risks in an investment bank have always come out of the revenues raised by those taking the risks. The big difference is that in the past these risk managers had far more power.

Historically, investment bankers in the City and on Wall Street worked in small partnerships, where management and owners mostly overlapped. Partners were personally liable and, while they earned wonderful amounts when things went well, their fortunes were on the line when they did not. In other words, there was a bonus but also a malus – a financial penalty if things went wrong. From the mid-eighties these partnerships began to list on the stock exchange, or were taken over by publicly listed commercial banks who wanted to take advantage of

deregulation and move into investment banking. Those commercial banks took over dozens of other banks and financial
institutions across the globe and consequently became 'too big
to fail.' In a relatively short time the ownership structure of
investment banks has radically changed. They are now publicly
listed themselves so the risk lies with shareholders rather than
partners, while bankers are paid partly in shares and options.
The higher the share price, the more their shares and options
are worth, and a really good way to way to raise that share price
is by taking more risk. And we've seen, what 'too big to fail'
really means is that the taxpayer will bear much of that risk.

There is an expression in the City for this new state of affairs: 'It's only OPM' – Other People's Money.

A front-office veteran whose bank was a partnership when
he started his career was very clear about how this difference in
ownership structure affects the way bankers operate. 'I was very
new and maybe a bit cocky,' he recalled. 'I thought I'd built
something very clever. So I went over to the head of trading
and showed it to him, saying, isn't this clever, look how we can
make a lot of money with this! The head of trading was a partner in the traditional sense. He looked at me and said: "Don't
forget, this is my money you're fucking with."' That was the
system back then, the veteran concluded. 'As a banker you had
the shareholder sitting next to you.'

It was genuinely eye-opening to realise just how recently
the investment banks and megabanks had mutated in this way.
You often hear that the problem with banks is that they take
excessive risk. But one look at the structure of banks is enough
to see that the real problem is the *ownership* of that excessive
risk. Those who take the risks are no longer the same people
who bear them. That fundamentally changes the role of risk
and compliance. The partners that they worked for in the past
had every reason in the world to fear a disastrous loss. That

meant power. In today's system, the risk and compliance department only serves to reassure the shareholders, regulators and taxpayers: those who shoulder the real risks.

Now I began to understand why the interviewees who worked in hedge funds, private equity and venture capital scoffed at the publicly listed 'too big to fail' banks claiming to be part of the free market. Capitalism without the possibility of failure is like Catholicism without a hell, they'd say. Or: 'Heads you lose, tails I win.' And: 'Banking today is like playing Russian roulette with someone else's head.'

I was still mulling this over when an intriguing message popped into my inbox: 'I'd be happy to discuss a part of banking that's not really seen.'

5

When the Call Comes

'It's amazing how fast the news spreads. A tidal wave of panic washes across a trading floor. When the call comes, people know right away. We may use the most innocent tone of voice, "Hi, could you pop up to the 20th floor for a moment?", but they know better. You never get an unexpected call from HR. Often, bankers just go missing when we ring. We need to deliver the message personally, and as long as we haven't done that, they can't be officially "put at risk of redundancy." So they disappear from their desks; they stop answering their phones. When they do come up, their faces have this deeply apprehensive look. Some of them bring a bag of their belongings packed as soon as they received "the call." People break down in tears, or they shout, or seem really confused. After our conversation, which typically lasts five minutes, they will be led out of the building by security. Especially the bankers who have access to sensitive stuff; they aren't allowed to touch their desks, their phones. We have caught people trying to copy files to a USB stick or sending details to their private email accounts. "They've got me now." That's what many say on their way out. Which is not very clever, incidentally, as it carries stigma. Much better to suggest you have gone on to a better job.'

It was one of those unusually mild autumn evenings when it is still pleasant to sit outside, and after a knowledgeable look at the wine list, the employee relations manager ordered a glass of Haut-Poitou Sauvignon Blanc. She was in her late twenties and had been working in human resources for a bank for a number of years. She explained that during that first five-minute conversation on the 20th floor many refuse to shake her hand or look at her, 'It's much easier to take out your anger on someone from HR who you don't know, rather than on your manager who you've worked with for any number of years. Managers will often join in the act, and blame everything on HR. Managers really hate this part of their job. Often they don't show up for the preparatory meeting. Can you imagine how annoying that is? We ought to role-play scenarios, go over the list and talk about cases that are likely to be difficult. Even if managers do show up for the preparatory meeting, they often forget all about our role-playing once we're in the meeting and simply say, "Look, you're at risk of redundancy. Now, over to her."'

Often people are too confused to take anything in. Sometimes she'll inform them that they may be deployed to another area of the bank. 'When we meet again, a number of days later, people often have no recollection of that conversation. At the second meeting we talk about redeployment, their new job, or we talk about severance pay, when there's no job. Some are very quiet, others really angry. They may have prepared themselves, spent a lot of time on Google to arrive at what is often an incorrect legal position. When someone is made redundant, it's all about money. Statutory rights stipulate we must pay up to £400 for every year worked at our bank. Except if you've been there less than two years, you get nothing. In the UK we tend to offer people far more, in exchange for which they must sign this document to promise that they're not going to sue. It's a form a blackmail and we call it "enhanced severance."' After a sip of her wine she continued, 'American managers find all of this terribly laborious. In the United States it's much easier to fire somebody.'

To conduct individual redundancy meetings like this on a nearly daily basis was 'a little soul destroying,' she admitted, but the large-scale waves of redundancies were worse. Her bank operated across the globe so the redundancies at each location all had to be announced within 24 hours. On days like that she may have 15 meetings, being on call from 7 a.m. until 10 p.m. 'You sit there trying to predict the next person's emotional response. Some of them really lash out; I have to be on my toes the whole time. It's exhausting. I become robotic, saying literally the same thing in every session. Managers comment on that, sometimes, but I'm like, what do you want me to do? This is the best way to say what I have to say.' Foreigners on a work-related visa must leave the country within 30 days of being made redundant. 'Imagine it – these people have friends, girlfriends, boyfriends . . . Often they have already spent the bonus they were expecting after New Year. Now they are not getting anything. One of the reasons people are laid off around autumn is that you don't have to pay them a bonus, and the pool gets bigger for those remaining.'

All this was food for thought. And not before long I had the chance to hear about the experience from the other side of the HR manager's table.

She was between 35 and 40 years old, having worked for well over a decade at a megabank, always in support roles. She had volunteered for an interview because she wanted to present a 'more realistic' and less negative side of megabanks. However, she kept on cancelling because 'things have been turbulent at work.' I kept on at her and finally we met in a nearly deserted coffee shop around 11 in the morning.

'It's hard,' she began. 'I worked between 10 and 15 hours a day, spending more time with colleagues than with friends or my partner. You become part of the fabric of the place. Then they dispose of you.' In the United States it's even worse, she added, and talked me through the process. In her bank a round of redundancies was referred to as 'the communications' and a day like that was crazy, she said, totally crazy. 'They start once everybody is in, around 7 to 7:30 a.m., and continue through-out the day. Everybody will be watching everyone else. Phones go off all the time – clients, internal or external calls – yet apart from that there is this eerie silence. When somebody gets up from their desk with their jacket and belongings you know it was HR on the line. If that person is popular or well respected, colleagues will break out into applause as they make their way to the HR meeting.'

When an entire team is made redundant the manager gets called up to HR first. The manager communicates to the team on an individual basis. Then the manager is made redundant. So a few months ago she had been sitting at her desk, nervously monitoring her manager. If he got up, she watched him. Turn-ing right meant the bathroom. Turning left meant HR. He turned left. A little later an 'undisclosed' number flashed on her phone. She said to a colleague: 'I am not answering that. I am not answering that.' But of course she did.

All in all, things went pretty much the way she had ex-pected. The first conversation was very short – five to 10 min-utes. She could tell they were trying to minimise the emotional impact of what had just happened to her, giving a blanket reason for her dismissal: 'the challenging marketenvironment'andthe-needfor'expense reduction.' A few days later she returned to be offered a severance package. She signed a 50-page document waiving all her rights. 'My package means I'm covered for a year.' After that first conversation they allowed her to go back to her desk to get her things in order. 'I think that was a gesture; I had been with the company for a long time.'

Immediately she sent an email to a colleague about a project they had been working on. 'I mean I didn't want things to go tits-up.' She had been preparing for this to happen, she explained, and in the weeks leading up to being made redundant she had cc-ed people on emails, so that they'd have the necessary information when she would no longer be there.

A silence fell and I ordered more coffee. So she had gone to great lengths to protect the bank from possible damage arising from her sudden dismissal? She nodded and said she was not bitter. In fact, in some ways it had been a relief. Her bank had had quarterly redundancy rounds for the past four years – since the crisis began. 'People constantly discuss the scale of what's to come,' she said. '"Do you think it's next Tuesday? It could be the day. Who do you think will go?" People sound out their managers. "Should I be preparing for anything?" Nobody feels safe, and it's not healthy. Morale is shit.' She repeated she was not bitter and really hoped to get back into banking as soon as possible: 'The combination of complexity and competitiveness, pace of change and like-minded people, together with the salary, makes the sector like no other.'

Did she have any regrets? She took her time to think. 'When you're on the list, you're on the list. I know that senior people stood up for me, but to no avail. My entire team was made redundant; there was nothing that could have saved me. You're a number. That's the deal you make when you go work in finance: you are a commodity.' She thought some more. 'This summer I turned down a pretty awesome job. Looking back I may have been overly loyal to my dysfunctional family – the bank I worked in.' A final swig of her coffee and she said almost cheerfully: 'I am not sure if this is a female thing, to be overly loyal, but it's definitely a mistake I'll never make again.'

This was certainly a 'part of banking that's not really seen,' as the human resources manager had put it in her email: people in the City can be out the door in five minutes. None of the bankers I had spoken to until that point had brought this up. But now that I began to ask about this aspect of the industry almost every new interview brought out another horror story. You get a call from a colleague: 'Look, could you do me a favour and get my coat and bag?' She is already standing outside with a blocked security pass. You return from lunch to find the desk next to you emptied out. You assume your colleague is on holiday until you see someone new is sitting at her desk. One moment you're working on a project, the next you're hugging each other and saying, 'Well, bye,' because the other is being led out of the building by security. In a meeting you suggest Natalie runs a particular test and your boss shakes her head: 'Natalie isn't here any more.' And this is how you learn that Natalie has been laid off. Or worse still, in the morning you swipe your pass only to hear a beep and find your entrance barred. You turn to the receptionist who says, after a glance at her computer screen, 'Would you please have a seat over there until somebody comes to fetch you?'

A junior dealmaker who had recently left banking of his own accord told me of a time when his bank suddenly 'let go' of a particularly popular colleague. 'It took everyone by surprise because this dude was not only very nice, professional and dedicated but he actually made a lot of money for the team. His eyes welled up and I'm sure he burst into tears when he left the floor. Moments after his departure, his desk was cleared and the head of our team got up to say something to the effect of: "He was a great guy but business is business and let's get back to work and make some money." So a guy you've spent X number of years sitting next to for most of your days since joining suddenly disappears and that's it . . . back to business. New faces spring up all the time. At first it's a bit weird. My boss used to say: "Every day you're getting closer to getting fired."'

Interviewees had a term for sudden dismissals of this kind: 'executions.' And there was more. Every year prestigious top banks such as Goldman Sachs and JP Morgan fire their worst-performing staff – no matter how much profit was made. It is called 'the cull,' the same term you use when infected cattle has to be destroyed, or farmers need to reduce the number of badgers on their land. 'Oh yes, we cull,' interviewees would say, or: 'When the cull comes . . .' A young dealmaker explained how his bank created their internal rankings system. Every six months everybody gets to evaluate their colleagues' performance in so-called 360-degree reviews, from 'excellent performer' to 'met expectations' all the way down to the ominous 'fails to meet expectations.' A system like this makes office politics very important, he had learnt. 'You need to say hello to the right senior people at the right time. Team members co-operate but they are also in competition for a better ranking in the review. As you would expect, friends will give friends good reviews.' Only three in 100 can be that 'excellent performer,' he added, while everybody knows that the bottom few per cent get 'chopped off.'

Stories and anecdotes like this sometimes made me conscious of how far Britain had travelled in the past 30 years. As a product of a typical north-west European country, I had been brought up to believe in the welfare state, job protections, safety nets and collective bargaining. These are now unfashionable notions in London's financial centre. My discomfort only grew when I heard the way investment bankers in the front office spoke of sudden dismissals. A round of redundancies was a 'reduction of headcount' or a 'clean-up of bodies' or 'bums on seats.' A senior investment banker said that in his department colleagues who had suddenly disappeared were always referred to as having resigned. It sounds better, he said with a shrug, and in one in 10 cases it's true. Compare the psychological mechanism to the way soldiers in a firing squad know that one of them is given a blank, he explained. If his colleagues are told someone was fired, they might think: 'Hey, that was a good guy and he still had to go. If that can happen to him it can also happen to me.' 'So we say "he resigned",' he said, 'implying he went on to an even better job.'

Machismo was the norm for bankers in the front office. Sudden dismissals separate the boys from the men, they seemed to say, and by taking it on the chin you show your mettle. Another recruiter I would meet over lunch every now and then compared the first time a banker is made redundant with a rite of passage, a ritual to be endured in order to gain membership to the tribe. 'Think of the young foot soldier in the Mafia who is nicked by the police for the first time. It is how you handle yourself that is important. If, like young Ray Liotta in *Goodfellas,* you do it right, you are part of the family.'

The flipside to this is that front-office investment bankers seem as disloyal to their bank as vice versa. Many of my interviewees had three or four banks on their CV by the time they were 35: jumping between jobs and banks frequently is the key to working your way up. There were countless stories of entire teams being poached, moving from one bank to another and sometimes back again – by which time everybody in the team is making vastly more than they did before the merry-go-round started.

The recruiters I spoke to confirmed that in the City this system of job-hopping is the norm, even more so in the boom years before 2008. A recruiter with over a decade of experience became a regular contact. His favourite lunch place was a traditional English pub in the historical heart of the Square

Mile. We chatted away over a pint and I got to grips with steak and kidney pudding. He explained that he gets approached by bankers who believe that they can make more money else-where, by banks with plans to move or expand into a particu-lar niche, and finally by banks who have just had one of their bankers poached by a rival. He remarked cheerfully that this gave recruiters a reputation for being 'parasites.' They earn their living from filling the gaps that their fellow recruiters create. He must have met over a thousand bankers in his career, he es-timated. 'Guys under 30 who make two or three million a year. I mean that desensitises you. It desensitises me. The other day I was talking to this banker who is quite good and makes only £150,000. I remember thinking, poor guy. He could be mak-ing double that, at least, if he moved to another bank. Then I caught myself: what do you mean, "poor guy"? He is making £150,000.

'People won't say, with my next move I want to make two million. They'll say they want to make "two bucks." And when they trade something worth two billion, they won't say that, they'll say "two yards."' He had noticed how traders tend to view everything through the prism of their work, including re-cruitment. 'They might say: "We had a bid out on someone, best guy in the street, but he didn't feel it was the right trade at this point in this career." So "bid" for job offer, "street" for the financial community, and "trade" for an actual job move.' I asked him about the most tense and exciting moments in a role like his. He knew right away: the moment a client has to hand in their resignation to their line manager. 'The candidate is led into a room and there the company will wheel out increasingly senior people who try to stop the candidate from leaving. This makes sense for the company; finding a replacement costs a lot of time and money. It's a significant disruption. It is a sound investment for a very senior person to come down and spend 15 minutes to stop this from happening.'

Recruiters beg candidates not to reveal the name of their new employer, he said, because the bank will bring in someone who used to work there. That person will say it's terrible over there, the job is not at all what it seems and so on. He found that first-timers nearly always give in to the pressure and tell their current employer where they are going. 'Afterwards they always tell us that this was their biggest mistake – staying silent on the matter can make the process far quicker and less painful.' Things can get pretty rough, he said, and told me about a candidate who returned to her desk after resigning to discover that everyone had been instructed to ignore her. She confided in a very good friend about her next job and that friend immediately briefed their manager. 'The ostracisation really got to her. One strike and you are out of the circle.' His impression was that women are bullied more than men when they resign, 'perhaps because women are believed to be more susceptible.'

•

In his classic book *Liar's Poker*, the American writer and former front-office banker Michael Lewis summarises the mentality behind this hire-and-fire system as: 'You want loyalty? Hire a cocker spaniel.' And why shouldn't bankers act like footballers and seek out the most prestigious or best-paying club? Particularly since the financial sector is extremely sensitive to the ups and downs of the economy; the easier banks can get rid of people in bad times, the more likely they are to hire them again when the economy swings back. That is the commonly accepted argument in favour of zero job security. In all the interviews, virtually no front-office bankers made the case for employment rights or any form of job protection. At the same time many spoke extremely negatively about the atmosphere in their banks and, digging deeper into the causes of the 'toxic culture,' they often hit on the hire-and-fire mentality. People are not appliances; a machine that might be discarded at any point is unaware of this fact and will function exactly like a machine that has a cosy spot reserved in the factory until the end of its days. Humans, however, are influenced by the awareness of their vulnerability and adapt their behaviour accordingly.

One risk and compliance officer I met for an al fresco lunch spoke without reservation of a 'climate of fear.' She was around forty, sardonic and straight talking. Having ordered a Cola Light and soup, she lit a cigarette, exhaled deeply and began to speak in rapid sentences: 'People need to speak to us openly and honestly. They must feel confident that we're not going to hit the panic button. Or call the regulators. Or move it up the hierarchy – same thing as hitting the panic button. Basically you need "off the record" conversations. Then you hear what's actually going on. But what usually happens when something goes wrong? We are the last to hear.' The 'fear factor,' as she called it, is very strong, she said, and there is very little trust. 'Think about your paycheck' is a standard expression. And: 'You don't want to rock the boat too hard.'

The first couple of weeks she remembered feeling the constant fear of being found out. The work was so complex and technical and jargon-laden and acronym-heavy. 'Some people are out to trip you up and undermine your authority, by asking an impossible question.' The first time she went into a meeting in the business area on which she was running some routine tests, she learnt a valuable lesson. As she brought out her notebook, her boss hissed, 'What are you doing?' 'Making notes,' she had replied. 'Don't,' he had said. 'People will clam up. You don't make notes in front of people. You write them later from memory.'

Another thing she learnt in those early weeks: never delete

emails. 'You want to form a trail so that when something goes wrong you're covered. I was like, well, when I make a mistake I don't mind taking responsibility for it, why be so defensive? But arse-covering is a major element if you want to survive in finance. Even when you've done nothing wrong, people may point the finger at you. Then you need your trail.'

She threw a glance at the other smokers sitting outside the restaurant and lit up another. In risk and compliance the culture of fear operates on two levels, she went on. 'It is very hard to get to the relevant information since everybody is afraid to share it. But even if they give it to you, you will think thrice before acting on it. You too are very easy to fire.'

Her salary was 'well under' £100,000, which she considered 'too much, absolutely, for what I'm delivering, which is of little value.' What keeps her in her job? Her face hardened. 'Money, if I'm honest, that's a big thing. And some colleagues. There are some terrific people I work with, real personalities. There's also the laziness factor. After spending an entire day behind screens, you are not going to go home and spend more time in front of your computer polishing up your CV and looking for jobs. 'This job involves in some part selling your soul for a good salary,' she continued. 'I am very troubled by that.

A lot of people aren't. No way will I reach retirement in a job in finance.'

Later, as we said our goodbyes, she breathed what sounded like a sigh of relief: 'It actually feels really good to get this off my chest.'

Many interviewees from the back and middle office came to the same conclusion: my bank suffers from a climate of fear. Fear of being tripped up, blamed, found out or fired.

Another compliance officer said that all the trading floors he had worked on in the past decade were in a 'permanent state of turmoil.' The cause? Wave after wave of redundancies. One time his team was told they were going to lose 12 people. 'Just like that,' he said. 'What baffles me: how is it possible that somebody just picks a number of how many people should be fired?' Just as revealing was the absence of any real resistance on the part of colleagues. 'So phlegmatic! Management told me: you need to bite the bullet, move on.' Ten per cent of the team were to be let go but nobody knew who it would be. 'Imagine the atmosphere on the day the telephone began to ring,' he said. In the end the decision was reversed and 40 people were added to his team. 'Without any explanation.'

The easier it is to fire someone, the easier it is for top managers to lose empathy, the Sauvignon Blanc-drinking HR manager had found: 'I have seen really senior people with massive flaws. They could nominate someone for redundancy on a whim. I am called in and I go, on what basis have you made that decision? In the next three days, as more information on that person comes in, it becomes clear that the senior person has made a huge misjudgment. Then, quite often, the very senior person will not back down, on principle. Humans become numbers very easily for them, it seems. They lose empathy.'

A risk analyst at a megabank with a PhD in theoretical physics had been to many protests and demonstrations against the financial sector, even attending Occupy London meetings in 2012. She characterised her bank as 'a collection of divisions engaged in permanent civil war . . . I was once pressured to fudge a set of numbers. If we didn't do this, we'd lose the trust of another division in the bank; we had to pretend that things were different from the reality. That's not easy, for a Christian like me. I managed to solve it by presenting the numbers differently. I got off without having to lie.'

'Intensely political' was another way people described their workplace. Everything you say can be used against you so you need to be on constant alert in case something can be taken out of context. Everybody is manoeuvring to look good. When somebody does make a mistake you get what people called 'feeding frenzies,' like when sharks smell blood. Then there is the malicious gossiping: 'What do you think of so-and-so?'

'There is such a blame culture,' said the penitent PR and communication officer. 'Three months after you leave your reputation is destroyed because it's easy to scapegoat the person who's not there.' It's even worse in the support functions like human resources, PR and communication and other areas of the back office, she added. 'I don't know why. And I hate to say it but women seem to be the quickest to point the finger.'

•

The more stories like this I heard, the more I began to feel something approaching almost sympathy for people in investment banks. But in addition to the personal ramifications of this fear and blame culture, the lack of job security has wider consequences for the working of the banks.

'The sector suffers from pervasive human capital destruction,' said the senior sales trader who characterised bonuses as 'theatre' and 'a ritual.' 'Someone new comes in and bang! He cuts headcount by 10 per cent. Now, if the economy doesn't really move and he gets the remaining 90 per cent to do all the work, then he looks smart. He has cut costs and kept revenue stable. But now the economy picks up and we're hopelessly understaffed. It's no way to run a business, but it's how many desks are run.'

The short-termism is endemic, agreed the rock-'n' roll trader. 'In my career I have almost never seen anyone trying to build something. There are just cycles of new guys coming in. They put forward a plan promising to make money in three or four years. The pressure is huge, and the easiest way is take more risk.'

Think of an election cycle, he said when asked for an example. 'You get new management coming in, they go over the numbers and decide: this desk doesn't work. They fire the senior guy and bring in a new guy, for *x* million. New guy kicks out four more guys, and brings in his own. When after three years it hasn't worked out, the bank fires those five, and it starts all over.'

There is one global investment bank, he said, which provides a notable exception to this culture: Goldman Sachs. This is what a lot of people don't realise about them, he added. 'You look at most guys at the top there, they are Goldman guys. There's actually less short-termism there – for me their consistent management is one of their great strengths.'

If you can be out of the door in five minutes, your horizon becomes five minutes. That was the essence of the stories about zero job security. Not only does all loyalty evaporate, but continuity does too. Nobody can build on anyone else; the best can be poached at any time, and meanwhile there are swords of Damocles hanging over everyone's heads: the waves, the executions and the yearly cull. What you end up with is the law – or rather the lawlessness – of the jungle. How realistic is it to expect 'internal controls' to do their jobs in such a context?

I put this to the compliance officer who had been told he'd be losing 12 members of his team. He was so concerned about being identified that I could not give any details about him, not even an approximation of his age. He was a regular reader of the blog and had written to say: 'I still don't think you understand banks.' When we met in his home I saw on his shelf *Fool's Gold* by anthropologist and *Financial Times* journalist Gillian Tett, probably the most highly regarded book to have appeared about the bankers who invented and built the complex products that blew up in 2008. According to Tett, the number-one problem in investment and megabanks is that everyone works in 'silos,' causing crucial information to get blocked rather than circulated.

Does that sound familiar? He nodded, adding that deep anxiety forces everyone to stay in his or her silo. 'My manager doesn't want me to have any contact with his superior, as he doesn't want that superior to have an alternative source of information. My manager needs to monopolise the information pipeline.'

He cleared his throat: 'We need to get rid of the idea of "the bank." That term implies a unity of action and purpose, as if there's an all-encompassing view driving that bank. There is no such thing. What we have is a collection of individuals in positions of power. Each of them manages his or her world. That's how they talk about it: "my world", or in some banks "my organisation." You don't work for the bank, you work for someone and he's got a world around him.'

This is why banks adopt new regulation in such a fragmented way, he thought. 'Everybody takes the bit that applies to his world.' And this is why waves of redundancies are so popular with ambitious managers. 'First, you prove to the people higher up: I can do this. I can take the heat and cut costs. Second, you can start making new hires, bring in people indebted to you. That's how you build a world.'

'We need to get rid of the idea of the bank.' That sentence stayed with me.

6

Every Man for Himself

Psychologists call them 'perverse incentives': rewards for undesirable actions or behaviour. As I spent more time among the bankers, I discovered more and more of these rewards and how they drove the dot-com bubble of 1999–2001. For a number of years around the turn of the century one group of investment bankers had been hyping up worthless internet start-up companies to their clients and the financial media. At the same time their colleagues in the same bank were generating huge fees by taking these companies public. How was that possible? The easy answer was 'greed' but look at the perverse incentives built into the system and a deeper logic emerges.

Traditionally, investment banking in the City and on Wall Street happened in firms that were partnerships, such as Goldman Sachs and Salomon Brothers in the United States and Cazenove (later bought by JP Morgan), Morgan Grenfell (bought by Deutsche Bank) and Samuel Montagu (bought by HSBC) in the UK. They had a reputation to maintain and often employed people for life. There were separate firms for trading, separate firms for asset management and separate firms for deal making or 'merchant banking': mergers, acquisitions and the listing of new companies on the stock exchange, known as 'Initial Public Offerings' or IPOs.

Since the 1980s all of these activities have been brought under the roof of one bank, after a wave of mergers and acquisitions within the industry. As a consequence an investment bank will be trying to achieve as high a share price as possible for the entrepreneur whose company it is taking public, while also advising investors whether that share price is a good deal. Meanwhile the asset management division has to decide whether to invest its clients' money in the newly listed company.

This is a conflict of interest of the highest order. Even more so when you realise that IPOs don't just bring in huge fees. When new shares are 'hot' and expected to jump in value as soon as they start trading, banks have the opportunity to pass them on to preferred clients – for example in exchange for other business. Or the bank can keep hot shares for itself, cashing in as trading starts.

The dot-com scandal originated in conflicts of interest of this kind and since then investment banks and investment banking divisions have been ordered to place 'Chinese walls' between their activities. Bankers who perform different functions within their investment bank cannot access each other's floors and they are not allowed to talk about business in the elevators. This way banks claim to be able to prevent the leaking of sensitive information and to avoid pressure being put on bankers in one section by bankers in another – for example, to lie to investors about the true value of a company being taken public by the bank.

Investment banks claim that their Chinese walls are enough to stop a banker who advises, say, BP and knows a lot about BP's plans for the future from sharing such immensely lucrative information with colleagues in sales trading – who make their money from persuading their clients to trade in . .

. BP shares. Or with colleagues in asset management who are looking to make a high return on the money entrusted to them by their clients – for example by trading in BP shares. Or with colleagues in 'prop trading' who are using the bank's own capital to make as much money as possible in the markets – perhaps by trading BP? And who are policing the Chinese walls? The middle office. Imagine *The Times* were to merge with a political lobbying firm and a PR consultancy company, only to declare: 'Dear readers, do not be concerned that we might change our reporting on politicians who are also clients at our lobbying and PR divisions. We have Chinese walls.'

Looking back I sometimes wonder how I could have held on to the idea for so long that the investment banks in their current form are basically OK. Perhaps it was a deep need for denial, while it is of course a venerable rule in anthropology to suspend judgment as long as possible. Once you have made up your mind it becomes very hard to keep it open.

So I kept going and began to observe an intriguing contrast. City workers look slick and suave but hearing the way many of them talked was unsettling – it was like listening to an exquisitely dressed football hooligan. The markets go up and down 'like a whore's drawers,' a mistake means you're 'fucked' and things do not go wrong but 'tits-up.' Without any apparent unease an interviewee would describe a lucrative deal or trade as 'rape and pillage' or 'slash and burn.' Militaristic terms abound: they 'worked in the trenches' while 'taking no prisoners.' Many remarked almost casually how in the world of finance it is 'have lunch or be lunch.' 'Sheep get slaughtered,' I was told, and given the chance you are to 'rip your client's face off.' Was this simply rowdy trading-floor humour? At one point in the fictionalised autobiography of a front-office banker, *City Boy*, the protagonist decides he needs to impress the big boys. So he saunters up to the dominant trader on his floor to ask him why he is 'such a fat bastard.' The reply: 'Because every time I fuck your wife she gives me a biscuit.' There are many such jokes and anecdotes making the rounds in the City. It is the nature of the beast, some would feel compelled to explain. Trading is zero-sum: I can only win if you lose and vice versa. 'There is a fool in every trade' is a standard expression. 'You have to know who the fool is, because if you don't, then you are the fool.' But that didn't explain why bankers in activities other than trading could be just as foul-mouthed.

Was there more to the tough-guy bankers' talk than bravado? What particular conflicts of interest, perverse incentives or underlying principles could explain this attitude? This question was gestating in my mind when in the spring of 2012 the aforementioned Greg Smith caused a global media storm by publishing a hard-hitting opinion piece on the op-ed pages of *The New York Times*: 'Why I am Leaving Goldman Sachs.' An executive director and head of the firm's U.S. equity derivatives business in Europe, the Middle East and Africa, he had worked on Goldman Sachs' trading floor in London for a few years. It was a 'toxic and destructive' environment, he wrote in his piece, adding that his colleagues referred to clients as 'muppets.'

Smith announced he was going to publish a book so I decided to interview some of his opposite numbers at competing banks. A handful of sales guys and builders of 'equity derivatives' were ready to talk – perhaps all the media attention in their area had riled them.

Some of them knew Greg Smith by name or in person and all of them asked: 'What is he talking about? He knows about caveat emptor, doesn't he?' There are different categories of clients, explained a structurer who built equity derivatives for a living. 'You have retail customers, ordinary people if you will, who are pretty well protected. Then you have professional investors or market counterparties and with them it's anything goes, really. The assumption is that professional counterparties should know what they are doing.'

'If you could sell your product for double the price, would you do it?' a second structurer of complex financial products asked. He believed that this is legitimate in business, provided clients have adequate information, adding that alongside this is 'an important rule' that clients ignore at their peril. 'You have got to read the small print. You need to bring in a lawyer who explains it to you before you buy these things.' Without a hint of irony he warned: 'Otherwise there is information asymmetry.'

In the 'real world,' of course, buyers are protected with numerous consumer rights laws. These allow purchasers the chance to return goods that are faulty or mis-sold, receive warranties on certain items or benefit from a cooling-off period on products bought through 'distance selling,' for example. In the financial world, however, 'caveat emptor' – or 'buyer beware' – is a perfectly normal and widely accepted legal principle for professional players. I pressed interviewees on the ethical aspect of all this and soon enough we hit the underlying principle: 'a-morality.' Please understand, everybody said: 'a-moral' is not the same as 'immoral.' Amoral means that the terms 'good' and 'evil' simply have no part in the decision-making process. In the City you do not ask if a proposal is morally right or wrong. You look at the degree of 'reputation risk.' Using loopholes in the tax code to help big corporations and rich families evade taxes is 'tax optimisation' with 'tax-efficient structures.' Financial lawyers and regulators who go along with whatever you propose are 'business-friendly,' cases of proven fraud or abuse become 'mis-selling' and exploiting inconsistencies between two countries' regulatory systems is 'regulatory arbitrage.'

Once you tune your ear in to it, examples abound, because the vocabulary available to people in finance to talk and think about their own actions is stripped of terms that could provoke an ethical discussion. Hence the biggest compliment in the City is 'professional.' It means you do not let emotions get in the way of work, let alone moral beliefs – those are for home. In most conversations the word 'ethic' came up only in combination with 'work,' referring to an almost absolute obedience to one's boss.

•

Some interviewees said they had needed time to adapt to finance's amoral culture. 'I remember that if I voiced an opinion based on moral considerations, I'd get looked at as if I were an alien,' said one former investment banker, while a risk and compliance officer recalled being branded a 'socialist' for asking about the social purpose of a financial product. Most interviewees, however, seemed to take the logic governing their sector for granted and pointed to the equally amoral hire-and-fire culture: this is simply how it works around here.

The pattern of scandals and crashes that had dominated the past few decades began to make more sense in this context. Consider what happened to the financial products developed in the 1970s to deal with increasing swings ('volatility') in the value of interest rates and currencies. Corporations, institutions and pension funds can be hit very hard by fluctuations of this kind so banks invented and developed derivatives that allowed these parties to protect themselves. This was a good idea that performed a useful service to the economy and society as a whole. But fast forward 20 years and what do you see? The British bank Barings collapses due to unsupervised and aggressive speculation by a rogue trader – using advanced foreign currency derivatives.

Second example: a company or government can go bust,

meaning investors lose their money. So a group of quants developed an insurance of sorts against default: the credit default swap or CDS. This was another good idea – but a good decade later, hyper-complex products using CDS hit the headlines when they played a crucial enabling role in the crash of 2008.

Finally: mortgages. These run for a long time and could be perfect investments for pension funds and other long-term asset managers. But as a pension fund you are not going to buy up individual mortgages. Enter another group of quants in the early 1990s who found a way to put lots of mortgages together and package them in a manner that made it possible for pension funds to invest in them. Again, this was a wonderful and bright thing to do . . . but a decade and a half later it was these products and their hyper-complex spin-offs that sank Lehman Brothers and others. How can valuable solutions to real problems derail and explode, time and again?

The financial sector is huge so there must be many factors at work at the same time – it is impossible to reduce such complex developments, spanning continents and decades, down to a single cause. Still, underlying those factors there was a recurring motif: amorality. If you can make a new financial product so complex that it becomes enormously profitable, and despite its opaqueness it remains within the law, who is going to stop you, inside or outside of your bank? For centuries the City was governed by the principle 'my word is my bond' and this is still the motto of the London Stock Exchange. Yet the underlying culture has changed beyond recognition and the tough banker talk seems to reflect this new order. Calling your clients 'muppets' creates emotional distance, making it easier to 'rip their faces off,' while all those 'fucks' prove to your colleagues that you have made the amoral mentality in finance your own.

•

Welcome to the world of globalised finance. In interviews, I began to bring up the subject of this amorality and challenge my respondents on the subject. In return, they offered three counter-arguments.

First, nearly every interviewee said: remember that amorality cuts both ways. Yes, profit is the only criterion, not how you make it. But it has to be done within the law. Remember that the organisational principle is amoral, not immoral. That means that in some areas the City is very progressive and much less clubbable than it used to be, partly as a result of its adherence to the letter of the law.

The days of 'my word is my bond' sound very attractive, those who had read up on the history of high finance would continue, and the veterans who remembered those days concurred. The City was much smaller, as were the number of clients, and so you had a high degree of social control. This meant cheating was likely to backfire on you, which was good. Not so good was that thanks to that same social control, a dominant group of white, male heterosexual men from the Christian upper-middle class were able to close rank and keep out women, Jews, gays and the working class. In *City Lives*, a collection of interviews published in 1996, top bankers and other financial figures talk about life in the City in the twentieth century. The open anti-Semitism, sexism, snobbery and homophobia among the generation over 70 years old puts paid to any nostalgia for the good old days. This, for example, is how George Nissen, who was born in 1930, described an attempt by the firm Smith Brothers to expand and break into new markets: 'They were strongly Jewish and regarded as rather spivvy. [. . .] It was thought you have to be very much more careful when you went to Smith Brothers than if you went to some other houses.'

Michael Verey was born in 1912 and for many years ran the Schroders bank: 'The only [gay bankers] I have known have, in fact, been unreliable. That's my principal recollection, they are unreliable *brokers*. You can't depend on them. You can't be sure. It very likely came out afterwards. First of all you realised they were unreliable and then later that they were homosexual.'

That was the City only one generation ago. Nowadays, things are different. The law bans discrimination so it has become taboo in investment banks. A Dutchman with roots in the South American former Dutch colony Suriname told me: 'In the Netherlands I will always be an *allochtoon* [a term used by white Dutch people to designate everyone else]. In the City nobody even seems to notice my skin colour.' Similar stories came from a German with Turkish grandparents and a Frenchman whose grandparents were Algerian. A young British Muslim was a few weeks into her bank's graduate programme and had just taken the scarf: 'It helps me keep perspective.' She hated her job but was struck by how tolerant and colour-blind everybody seemed. 'The City is actually ridiculously tolerant. It's quite amusing; I think people are wooed by me. And they're overly nice about the scarf, asking: do you shake hands? I have to say, this is really nice and quite different from my experiences in continental Europe.'

I may have run into the lucky ones but none of my interviewees from a 'minority' had encountered open discrimination at their banks. The glass ceiling is as intact as it is elsewhere in society, yet two women at brokerages said independently that they preferred working with bankers as opposed to, say, fellow brokers or clients. 'The big banks have diversity policies so it's not just white straight males you meet there,' said one. The other believed 'investment bankers are so terrified of law suits that they would rather bite off their tongue than say something sexist.' A back-office worker said her bank was 'fully aware of the laws on sexism and discrimination. In my mind they are really trying too hard. There's always some scheme or stand over-promoting the next workshops for mothers-to-be. One week it's Diversity Week, the next it's I-don't-know-what Week . . .'

Amorality ensures a level playing field, according to interviewees. What's more, they added: it is not like banks have a choice. This brought us to the second counter-argument that came up in the interviews. Amorality as an organising principle is imposed on us and enforced by shareholders, who look at returns and returns only. The term here is shareholder value, essentially a doctrine holding that companies listed on the stock exchange must be judged by one criterion: the value they create for their owners, the shareholders. The rock-'n'-roll trader needed only a few sentences to sketch the straitjacket: 'If you are a pension fund with shares in Morgan Stanley, and you see that Goldman Sachs made 50 per cent more profit, you will not like that. These numbers make you look like a bad investor. So you put pressure on Morgan Stanley, saying, "You have 18 months to prove you can turn this around or there'll be a sell-off."' This logic then trickles down the organisation. Under the CEO sit the global heads with the overall responsibility for a particular activity or region. 'Global heads of banks know: I have to make x billion in the next 18 months or I'm out. They can't say: "It's going to be difficult for the next five years." The market demands results, from banks as much as from any other company.'

'The truth is that every year you have to bring in more revenue,' says former investment banker Rainer Voss in the widely acclaimed confessional documentary *Master of the Universe.* 'Management does not care if things have changed, if a particular market has become less lucrative, this year or structurally.

Ten per cent more revenue, every year – I don't care how you do it.'

All corporations listed on the stock exchange are subjected to this regime. That was the third counter-argument offered by interviewees: banks are like any other major corporation in the world today. Quite a few readers of the blog working for non-financial multinationals agreed and wrote emails to tell me that the behaviour and mentality I'd described were pretty similar in their jobs – even including the language.

A man in his early thirties had made the switch from a multinational consumer goods company to the antipoverty activists of Oxfam. Asked why he had left a well-paying job at a prestigious corporation he said: 'The culture was super-competitive, all about crushing our competitor. I just didn't buy into the company's mission, that all that mattered was how to sell more stuff, how to design shampoo pumps that gave out more shampoo than the customer needed so that they'd end up buying more shampoo.' A reader who had been with a global software giant for many years told of a weekend when the entire global sales force was flown to Las Vegas. 'The best performers would be invited to come on to the podium to be honoured. But first we were shown about 10 minutes of a war movie, when this guy stepped forward and began shouting: "We are gonna rip the skin off competitor X!" And we'd be expected to go, fists pumping in the air, "Yeah!" Next he shouted: "We are gonna fuck over competitor Y!" and we'd go, "Yeah!"'

•

Welcome to the real world, investment bankers would sometimes tease me as they saw me struggle with the fact that in the City all relations are recast as transactions: between shareholders and the bank, between the bank and its employees, between banker and client.

It took a while for it all to click but of course, why would bankers treat their clients better than they are treated themselves, by their own bank and by the bank's shareholders?

The Sauvignon Blanc employee relations manager had often witnessed how from one day to the next headquarters could announce a 5 per cent 'headcount reduction' – another sterilising term to describe sudden mass lay-offs. 'I go over the list with managers. Women on maternity leave are often the first to go. People who are absent due to illness.' The logic is inexorable: lower costs mean higher profits and hence more shareholder value.

This is an environment where it is everyone for themselves, people would say, often with a shrug. 'I could tell you crazy stories about people being dragged from the toilets, from hospital, from holidays . . .' said the former PR and communications officer. 'A colleague would get a call at 2 a.m. from her boss in New York: "Send me X right away!" So she says: "I already sent it to you." Reply: "Well, whatever, send it again."' Since they are mostly judged on results, not on how they achieved them, so 'the most demanding people are the most successful.' In her career she had seen many people get promoted. 'All of them would say they wanted to remain human. But those that managed to didn't do that well. The others would change, often overnight. On Friday they were a human being, on Monday they turn into this shouting and screaming person. When I left, people said: "Now you'll go back to the real world, with real people." They are not real people, in banks. Some banks are worse than others in this.'

Investment banks burn through people, she concluded almost matter-of-factly. 'There's logic to it. If you can't take the pace or the culture you're not going to last. Some of those people just don't get it and are resentful afterwards. Others are happy to go off and do something different; open a restaurant or a B&B or sail round the world, whatever.'

•

Would City workers want it any other way? Some interviewees said they would happily trade part of their 'compensation' if that meant the bank would treat them better. But particularly in the front office the almost unanimous verdict was: look, this is how the world works. If you can't stand the heat just get out of the kitchen.

Insiders seemed to have 'internalised' the system's logic, as psychologists call it, and how far this goes became apparent when, six months after his sensational resignation letter in *The New York Times*, Greg Smith published his book on Goldman Sachs.

In it he explained that for clients there is tremendous potential for profit in the kind of structured derivative products that Goldman Sachs sell. As well as tremendous potential for short-term loss. The trick is to bury the necessary warnings about possible downsides 'in the fine print of the 10-page disclaimer at the end of the contract. Most clients pay as close attention to that as you do when you hit the "Accept" button before downloading music from iTunes.'

Suppose, Smith wrote, that you buy a can of tuna to find that it contains dog food. What a nasty surprise, did the label on the can not say tuna? You turn to the legal document that came with the tuna and there it says 'can also contain dog food.' The governments of Italy and Greece, the Libyan sovereign wealth fund, the American state of Alabama and 'countless other endowments and foundations' . . . over the past years all of them discovered dog food in their Goldman Sachs-made can of tuna, Smith wrote. This is immensely profitable, he added, especially with the category of clients Smith described as those 'Who Don't Know How to Ask Questions.' In his time there, Goldman Sachs kept an internal list of clients that had brought in the most commission. 'There is something highly disconcerting,' Smith writes, 'about seeing a global charity or philanthropic organisation or teacher's pension fund in the top 25.'

'It was all too much,' Smith concludes in the final chapter of *Why I Left Goldman Sachs*. 'We had advised Greece all those years ago how to cover up its debt by trading a derivative. Now that the chickens were coming home to roost, we were showing hedge funds how to profit from Greece's chaos; and on the other side of the Chinese wall, our investment bankers were trying to win contracts from European governments to advise them how to fix the mess.'

That was why Smith had quit his job and taken the career-destroying decision to blow the whistle. It was explosive stuff. Here was someone naming names. But the response from the sector was one of relief or even boredom. Smith had merely described perfectly legal practices that were covered by caveat emptor.

Many in the financial press took the same line and so it was not Goldman Sachs but Greg Smith who had to defend himself. The most prominent financial journalist at *The New York Times*, Andrew Ross Sorkin, went so far as to declare that in hindsight Smith should not have been given the opportunity to publish his resignation letter on *The New York Times* op-ed pages in the first place. The book was boring, Sorkin said on TV, and 'not particularly revealing.'

What was shocking here was how little anyone within the industry was shocked.

7

Islands in the Fog

'There are arseholes and idiots in every profession. I'm pretty sure journalism isn't immune. Bankers get tarred with the behaviour of a few. It's a witch-hunt. Replace the word "banker" with "Jew" and you see what I mean. The vast majority of those working in financial services are decent, honourable people doing decent and honourable things. Finance weeds out the arseholes, idiots, charlatans and fools pretty quickly and that's the main reason I don't recognise the picture painted by many of the contributors to your blog. Maybe they are some of the ones who have been weeded out?'

Criticism of this sort appeared under virtually every interview, always from people presenting themselves as insiders and often accompanied by the suggestion that the blog was a cheap attempt by the *Guardian* to score points with lefty readers. Obviously, I was concerned about the reliability and representativeness of the sort of people who risk their job for an interview – 'selection bias' in social science-speak.

Whether interviewees were who they said they were was quite easy to check on social media such as LinkedIn. Verifying their stories was a different matter, frustratingly, because

I was not allowed to observe anyone working in the banks. However, the most important things *in* their stories could be substantiated: the existence of caveat emptor, zero job security, the dangerous logic of 'too big to fail' and the implications and pressures of a listing on the stock exchange. It was clear that these conflicts of interest and perverse incentives are real, even if it came to light that each and every interviewee I spoke to was a delusional fantasist. A year into my research the blog was beginning to feel like an organisational detective. First I had been looking into the *who-dunnit* and the *why-dunnit* but anybody who reads too many police novels will tell you that an investigator looks beyond motives. So what was the *how-dunnit*? What opportunities for abuse – legal as well illegal – exist within banks? How does the architecture of today's megabank make abuse so easy and likely?

Such a question is impossibly broad so I had to rephrase it. Suppose that the big investment banks and megabanks are serious about fundamentally changing their culture, as they have claimed to be doing on numerous occasions since the crash . . . is it even possible for the top management have enough of a grip on the organisation to make that change?

A number of interviewees were struggling with this very question on a daily basis, and our conversations inevitably turned to complexity, and to the profound changes brought to the world of finance over the past decades by 'quants.'

In the middle office, quants build or manage the models their bank uses to calculate and possibly neutralise ('hedge') its risks. Drawn from academic backgrounds in maths, physics, chemistry and biology, these wizards invented the products that played a key role in the crash. Renowned quant Emanuel Derman typifies this new breed. After a few years as a physicist in academia and AT&T Bell Laboratories, Derman went to work for Goldman Sachs in 1985. In his bestselling autobiography

My Life As a Quant he writes: 'In physics you're playing against God. In finance, you're playing against God's creatures.'

The explosion of complexity across the financial sector is crucial to understanding the current state of the City, the interviewees said, so I was fortunate to find quants among the volunteers. Four in particular stood out.

My first quant worked in 'high frequency trading' at a hedge fund. We met at the Royal Exchange Grand Café near Bank tube station, right in the historical heart of the City. He was around 35 and wore jeans and a T-shirt; as a computer programmer he never saw clients anyway.

'Compare the movements of shares on the stock market with waves,' he explained over a cola. 'Our company is like a surfer trying to spot a wave, ride it for a tiny moment and get out again before it breaks.' On any given day his computers bought and sold the same share tens of thousands of times, holding it for very short periods of time – sometimes mere milliseconds. Ever since he could remember he had loved maths, he said over his second cola. He is drawn to 'the precision and beauty of it. An answer is either right or wrong. So it's really very ironic for me to have ended up in this one area of maths that is all about correlations and approximations.' Imagine my luck, he continued happily: 'What would I have been doing with my maths skills 100 years ago? Or 100 years from now? This is exactly the right time in history to have these skills. And I have them.' High frequency trading is not something that was once done by humans and is now handled by computers, the programmer explained. 'No human being, or collection of human beings, could do the volume of trades computers are doing at the moment at stock exchanges across the world. This is something new altogether.'

'Something new altogether' is a phrase one hears frequently inotherareasinfinance, too. Anothergoodexample of someone working in a new sector was my second quant. He was in his late forties, an inconspicuously dressed man with a crushing handshake. We met in Canary Wharf for lunch, in his case pasta. He had spent over a decade at a big investment bank before moving to a financial software company. When I asked him for a job description he said simply: 'Quant.' Could he give an example of how a quant like him was different to me? His face broke into a grin. 'If I look out my window and I see three boats coming down a river, I am automatically going to calculate how they'll avoid collision, which will pass which, when and where. In traffic I drive my partner insane by doing manoeuvres that she finds terrifying, because she hasn't made the calculations about other cars' speed and direction that I have.'

At the moment he was developing a 'neural network' or 'self-learning algorithm' to identify fraudulent transactions. 'Say you buy your wife a £30 bouquet of flowers on Friday at 1 p.m. in London. Now if you do the same thing next Friday, the model will begin to understand that this is normal behaviour for the card. If you then suddenly try to withdraw €3,000 from an ATM two minutes later in Mozambique, the model will generate an alert. The cardholder is protected from anxiety, the bank is protected from loss and – assuming that the bank's fraud team are on the ball – the person who has fraudulently obtained the card details might find himself or herself coming to the attention of the police. Everyone's happy.' I asked about the nature of the work he used to do on the trading floor of an investment bank. 'Traders are the warriors of our world,' he said after some thought. 'They go out and fight. I think of them as egos on legs. Sharp suits, looking very smart . . . We quants are the trader's brain. It's our model that defines not only the risks the trader can take, the model also calculates how much risk he is taking with his particular trades at any given moment.'

These were not happy years, on the trading floor, he said.

'I am just not enough of an arsehole to make it there. You have 1,000 vice-presidents vying for 10 managing director posts. People will do anything to get ahead – backbiting, backstabbing, the whole nine yards. For those of us who find life surrounded by other people difficult enough as it is, the requirement to network is hellish.'

After completing his PhD he worked on the Large Hadron Collider at CERN in Geneva. 'Many people I know from back then are still at universities, doing research and climbing the slippery slope to professorships and fellowships. They work the same astonishing long hours as I do, yet get paid a fraction. From a purely scientific perspective, they get to do some really, really interesting work. I often say, only half jokingly, that I "sold my soul." I make a little over £200,000 a year, including my bonus.' He believed that he had 'sacrificed a marriage on the altar of work' and a few years ago he had found himself 'taking advantage of psychiatric services.' These days he was taking a large dose of daily medication 'to try to stabilise myself.' He has mild Asperger's syndrome, he said, not identified until adulthood, which made everything particularly difficult. 'I find it hard to switch off. It's very tempting to just stay in the world where everything can be understood in mathematical language.'

Since he ate as fast as he spoke his pasta was long gone and for the first time a silence fell. Then he said, only half mockingly: 'I'm quite certain that I'm going to end up as one of the single old blokes that you might occasionally come across – nice, big house in the country, lots of dogs, materially comfortable and yet utterly alone and mad as a fish.'

The divide between quants with and without Asperger's was a recurring theme in the interviews: it seemed those with the syndrome tended to go down in the treacherous waters of their bank. One cold English morning I met another quant who clearly struggled with the complexities of human negotiations. Waiting for him in Starbucks, as we'd agreed via email, I was approached by a man who said abruptly: 'We are meeting, aren't we? Listen, I talk really fast and have a mild form of Asperger's. This means I am not good at picking up on facial expressions and nonverbal communication. If there is something you don't understand you have to say so, OK?'

For an instant I was genuinely speechless and sort of nodded, making the very mistake he had warned against. Only then did I say: 'I have understood, thank you.'

He was around 30 years old, the son of poor Asian immigrants, and he insisted that the suit he was wearing that day was his only one. He explained that his maths skills had got him a scholarship for one of the best private schools in the land, followed by a place at a top university. 'I was very bored there.' With a complete lack of false modesty, he listed his superior qualities and spoke about his role: 'I am not lacking in confidence.' After a few years at an investment bank he was an investment strategist with a smaller financial firm, offering investors 'big picture' advice. 'As a strategist you will, for example, look at the average increase in salaries in the United States. You discover it's been essentially flat; people make the same year on year. Then you look at consumption, which was growing every year. You ask, how is that possible? Answer: debt. Is that sustainable? No, you cannot live beyond your means indefinitely. New question: has the market priced this in – meaning, do prices reflect that this can't go on? Answer: no, they haven't, even after the dramatic falls we've seen. You can then look at historical precedent: how does a country return to a sustainable course, and how painful is that going to be?'

You learn to be humble in this job, he said. A while back a firm put out this very good report, he explained, and on page five they wrote: 'Whoever rips this page out and sends it to us gets £50.' They ended up paying out only £250, he said. Apparently few of their other clients had got as far as page five of the report as investors are deluged with information daily. 'Am I going too fast?' he suddenly asked, only to resume firing off one observation after another – each so precisely formulated that my pencil couldn't keep up with him. Basically he was working every waking hour, he continued. 'Always reading stuff. It can drive my wife mad – but she still loves me. I thoroughly enjoy my job as it is all about understanding how the world works and helping others understand it, too. What could be more fun?'

He had been making around half a million pounds a year at his investment bank, only to leave of his own accord for a big pay cut. The problem is that banks make their money from optimism, he explained. He was convinced that nothing structural had been done to fix the sector after the crash of 2008. Instead everyone was taking on new debt to pay off older debts. 'It's like drinking your hangover away with ever more drinks. You are destroying your liver. That's what's currently happening.' He was pessimistic, in other words, and this was a problem for his bank. 'If you are going to tell investors that the economy is going down, they will move their money somewhere safe and reliable such as cash. It is tricky to charge fees for trading or managing cash. It also becomes more difficult to convince investors to purchase riskier products.' So he had no regrets about leaving, he said. He believed that in banks 'three out of four promotions come from networking, not how good you are at your work. I am a horrible networker. I can speak to big crowds but I feel very uncomfortable in one. Though I am working on it, small talk is still very difficult for me. Plus, I don't drink alcohol.'

Every quant with Asperger's said the same thing: people like us do not survive in investment banking. However, if you are a quant without Asperger's, the world of finance is at your feet. The best illustration of this is someone I nicknamed the 'super quant.' As a senior managing director at a top bank he had been making multiple millions for a number of years only to move to a hedge fund where his pay was even higher. Quants like me are geeks, he said. 'I'm fine with that word. We've absorbed it, the way homosexuals have with "gay" and journalists with "hacks." Even 10 years ago there was far less respect for us. Now we are highly prized. Finance today is about technology and data, so technologists and people who understand maths and data are paid very, very well.'

Before his recruitment by the bank in the early 1990s he too had worked at a university. His preconceptions of an investment bank were based on two famous books he had read: *Liar's Poker* and *Barbarians at the Gate*. 'Traders as loud, crass, badmouthed, macho dickheads. The sort of guys with red braces who shout "buy, buy, sell, sell" into their phones and have eating competitions.'

Many outsiders still seem to believe that these are the guys in banks taking the big positions, and with it the big risks, he said with a hint of contempt. 'That's over. Some of the best traders are now women. Totally unassuming, cerebral and talented. Trading is no longer a balls job. It's a brains job. To be sure, the kind of maths traders now have to be able to do is not of the wildly hard variety. But it requires real skills in that area.'

This is the revenge of the nerds, some successful quants would say: the intelligence that isolated us as children in the playground now brings us money and status. This category of quants could sound genuinely relieved at having found their place in the world, whereas the old guard seemed to be struggling. Traditionally, brokers treat traders to extravagant nights out in exchange for business. 'Suddenly I am having to take out a 24-year-old maths nerd,' a broker said, shaking his head.

'Taking him to the hottest clubs, ordering the best champagne. A boy like that has never properly partied in uni, hardly any experience with alcohol, still figuring out the girl thing . . .'

It was a humorous image. But the conversation grew more serious when people in 'internal controls' began to explain the three ways in which the rapid increase in complexity had made their banks extremely vulnerable – if not downright unmanageable.

First of all there is immense scope for misunderstandings. The super quant had had to deal with quite a few bankers in higher management who simply could not follow the maths: 'In banking, nobody who is any good at his job says: "this is true" or "this is certain." You speak in probabilities. Or you should. The trouble is, many non-quants don't think in probabilities, or statistics. Say I look at a portfolio of trading positions in the market and I tell you that there is a one in 100 chance of losing £5 million tomorrow.' He looked me in the eyes: 'Now what did I just tell you? I told you that one in every 100 days you are going to lose at least £5 million. But many non-statistically trained people misinterpret this and think I told you that you can't lose more than £5 million. Those same people won't realise that I didn't say anything about the losses with a chance of one in a thousand or one in a million.'

A professor in financial mathematics at a top university in London was a quant himself and had seen many of his students take up jobs in the City. Suppose, he said, that a group of quants develops a financial product based on a model they have built. And suppose senior management are not quants themselves. In that case 'senior management doesn't really understand what is being pitched to them. How can they ask the right questions about the assumptions underlying the model, about the model's vulnerability to yet unknown and unknowable factors, or about the data set of the past 10 years used to project the product's revenue?' Remember, too, that the quants may very well lack the social skills to explain things, he went on – for instance because they have a mild version of Asperger's. 'What senior management hears is this: we have this great product, and had we had it 10 years ago, we all would have made a lot of money.'

Misunderstandings are dangerous but at least as frightening are miscalculations – when quants themselves no longer comprehend what is going on. Consider the high frequency trading that the first quant worked in. 'When there is a crisis you really realise just how strange and evanescent these programmes are,' said a compliance officer who used to work on a trading floor. 'How do we access them? No human being can see what high frequency trading does. We can only see it afterwards, when it has already made its impact.'

As a last resort people actually rip the cable out of the computer if things start to go wrong, the compliance officer went on. 'I've seen that happen, but it seems ridiculously primitive in such technological environments.'

A number of back- and middle-office workers claimed to have witnessed high frequency trading computers being disconnected: after a tsunami, an unusually large terrorist attack or the sudden prospect of a Greek default.

What if the plug cannot be pulled in time? In the 'the flash crash' on May 6, 2012, share prices suddenly lost hundreds and hundred of points in a matter of minutes. Then, as quickly and inexplicably as they had crashed, prices recovered – while the world of finance looked on in terrified bewilderment. Complexity can render even insiders helpless, explained the 'head of structured credit' at a big bank. In his mid thirties, slightly restless but quick to laugh, he is one of the most good-natured people I have met in two years of researching. We met on a grey day in January for lunch. After fighting the urge to order a glass of cider he settled on alcohol-free ginger beer and a pork pie.

'Those were scary times,' he said about the days, weeks and months after the collapse of Lehman Brothers in 2008. 'You think: we are in a new paradigm. Nothing works the way it used to. My department's potential losses were hundreds of millions of pounds and several billions across the whole of the bank. We began to realise: this could sink the bank. If the market had crashed further we would have gone down.' His job had been to manage a computer program that bought and sold financial products in order to neutralise risks the bank ran on other products. In the years before 2008, he said, the *Financial Times* would sometimes call people like him the 'F9 model monkeys' after the key you press to 'get the algorithm to tell you how things are going; what the value is of your portfolio. "Monkey" alluded to the fact that some of us didn't understand what the algorithms did.'

The *Financial Times'* hunch proved correct during the crash. The algorithm ran on a model based on assumptions that no longer held in the autumn in 2008. In the years before, his team would know in their heads to within a few thousand what profit or loss they had made for the day. Then they would press F9 and have it confirmed by their systems. 'When the crisis hit we would press F9 and get a number that was totally unexpected. We'd ask: how can we have lost so much money? What happened?'

In the old days they would send a daily report about their profits and losses upstairs and hear no more about it. Now his report was pored over by 10 risk managers in London, then 20 more in his bank's parent country. 'This was enormously stressful,' he said. 'You really don't want to be caught out by a risk manager in headquarters. Because that risk manager won't go back to you, they'll go straight to the board.'

What was much more stressful still was that most people in the bank didn't understand our products, he continued. 'Even the risk and compliance people who were supposed to be our internal checks and balances . . . We had to teach them how to monitor us.'

Those high up in an organisation know just enough for the role they are in, he had discovered, adding: '"Just enough" is not enough in an emergency. . .' For hours he would be on the phone to people of increasing seniority. 'I realised, they don't understand, not on a fundamental level. They will not be able to spot a mistake, correct us when we fuck up, or take an informed decision. It was down to us, and I was losing precious time talking to the top people. And to their underlings. This was when I would explode; when people would be sent to me with a question they did not themselves understand. I would tell them, "Look, you're adding no value. If you tell me you don't understand the question you're asking me, that's fine. I will sit down and explain. But how can my answer to your question be of any value when you don't even understand what you're trying to get me to tell you?"'

Those days had taught him valuable lessons about human nature. 'The arse-covering was extraordinary. At one point we worked out a solution. We'd have to take another loss but then the thing would be back under control. We propose this and it gets shot down.' The bank did not want to acknowledge more losses at that point, and chose to let it fester and face considerably bigger losses later on. This was when his team had begun to email *everything*, purely to cover themselves: 'As discussed in meeting X, this is our proposal. I am strongly encouraging . . .' They knew the top wouldn't go for it but they were not sending these emails to the top. They were sending them to potential investigators and prosecutors of the future.

I asked about any positive memories. 'The team spirit,' he said without hesitation. 'There were only a handful of us, like a Swat team, all from different countries because that's the

City of London for you. And the environment was intellectu-
ally challenging, to put it mildly.' It helped that he wasn't the
one who had traded the products blowing up in their face. The
products lost his bank a lot of money and his clients too. But he
could be fairly dispassionate about this: 'It hadn't been me who
sold them the products.'

His pay in the year before he left his bank was £400,000
including bonus. This is not bad for somebody who entered the
bank at 18 and worked his way up, all the way from the back
office, he said. 'I was the only one in my high school who did
not go on to university. It was not for me. I fell into this business. And I don't think I was in it for the money; when I was in
high school my parents tried to bribe me into working harder.
I never did.'

His laughter sounded uneasy. 'My employers practically
threw the money at me – I didn't ask for any of it! Every bonus time that come around they'd say, "We're paying you a
bit more than we guaranteed. A gesture of our thanks." In the
same breath they'd say, "And for next year your guarantee will
be X." Not once did I ask for more . . . How could I? They were
paying me a lot of money.' It was weird, he acknowledged: his
pay really started to escalate during the crash. 'This was a bomb
and I was basically the only one who could defuse it.'

Still, being known to be working in finance was not great,
in those days. 'Nobody in my social circle was in banking. My
mother would feel compelled to defend me when somebody
said something about bankers. Friends turned on me, on my
wife. I would go to a party and I'd get fried by a socialist friend
ripping into bankers.' A little under a year later he had left the
bank. He was still 'nursing' himself, as he put it. The night
sweats are gone but not the skin condition. 'It was stress. My
granddad was a diligent milkman and my dad a diligent po-
liceman. I was just being diligent in an industry that throws its

money around.'

Complexity vastly increases the scope for misuse and even abuse. Whether the crash of 2008 was ultimately down to that or to a huge misunderstanding – Dr No or Dr Nitwit – is still the subject of heated discussion. But no such controversy exists surrounding the scandal caused by the trader known now as 'the London Whale.' In the spring of 2012, a trader at the London offices of JP Morgan by the name of Bruno Iksil managed with his small team to run up a $6.2 billion loss. The nickname refers to Iksil's humongous positions – in other words he had put a vast amount of the bank's capital at risk.

Iksil was based in the City but JP Morgan is an American bank so the Senate's Permanent Subcommittee on Investigations began to dig into this 'monster loss.' Iksil could not be summoned to the United States, but the people working in JP Morgan's internal controls could.

When they got wind of the risks Iksil was running they had demanded an explanation: how was he going to get their bank out of this? His answer was simple: 'Sell the forward spread and buy protection on the tightening move, use indices and add to existing position, go long risk on some belly tranches especially where defaults may realise, buy protection on HY and Xover in rallies and turn the position over to monetise volatility.'

Could you tell us what this means? the committee members asked the JP Morgan risk managers. Nobody was able to do so. JP Morgan is considered the bank with possibly the best risk management in the world. In the year before his whale-like loss, Iksil's pay came to $7 million. Iksil didn't break any laws and has never been prosecuted.

The London Whale cost JP Morgan a lot of money but banks can also use complexity as a deliberate tool for their own purposes. I spoke to a restructurer who advises small companies in financial difficulty so that they can meet their debt obligations to his bank. He often felt overwhelmed by the complexity of the products and instruments his bank had sold to 'his' companies. 'Sometimes it looks like witchcraft to me,' he said. 'I have to comb through all that, dozens of different instruments, dozens of different kinds of bonds issues. Many of these financial products are bespoke, put together by the bank specifically for the client. The good thing is that allows for nuance and it can be tailored to the circumstances and unique needs of the company. The problem is the lack of clarity.'

Larger businesses do understand the financial instruments they are buying, he had found. Smaller companies may understand part, but they will not know the full ramifications. 'So we come in, look at what they've bought, and try to explain. Then, when top management discover what they have bought, there's anger and frustration. They are responsible, and they know it. At the same they were pressured into buying these instruments by our sales teams.'

The fewer people who understand what is going on, the more room there is for misunderstanding, miscalculation and abuse. And to make this worse: accidents in today's financial world can become very expensive very quickly – as the adventures of the F9 monkey or the London Whale show. Potential losses on some complex financial products are almost limitless. When extending a loan or buying shares, you know in advance your maximum losses, i.e. the amount involved. Many complex products, however, are like an open-ended insurance policy. You agree with an airliner that on January 1 next year you pay out a set amount for every dollar that the oil price exceeds a certain level. If on New Year's Eve the oil price ends up below that level you collect your premium – like a travel insurer who does not need to pay out after a problem-free holiday. But if instead the oil price has risen you have to pay. The point is that the oil price can go up a long way, and with it your losses.

Bankers are correct to point out that virtually all multinational corporations are publicly listed and therefore subject to the amoral regime of shareholder value. However, a handful of employees in a division somewhere at Shell or McDonald's are highly unlikely to cause their company a few billions in losses. At investment banks this is a very real possibility, as former investment banker Rainer Voss says in the *Master of the Universe* documentary: 'I cannot think of another industry where one individual can lose his company so much money.' Think of an upsidedown pyramid, he explained, since: *'Die Leute die richtigen Schade anrichten können, die sitzen unten'* – 'those who build or trade the explosive products are sitting very far from the top.'

•

When a small group of people can lose billions with activities that are extremely hard to monitor because of their complexity, you would expect internal controls to want to be on top of things. Except that this is close to impossible, interviewees explained. 'As a CEO you cannot understand every single algorithm your bank uses, every product they trade,' said an external accountant who had just audited the books of a large financial institution. 'CEOs get someone telling them, "Don't worry, it's under control."'

The way an internal accountant defended her CEO was even more troubling. This was the young woman who found it so difficult to get a job outside the sector. She was working for a megabank in group financial reporting, the division that 'pulls the numbers together across the bank,' as she put it, for the quarterly and yearly reports among others. 'We look at variations month-on-month and year-on-year, and we construct a narrative why income went up or down. This is fed straight to the bank's chief executives.' She had the levelheadedness and calm confidence you often find among accountants and people responsible for 'the numbers.' A few times during the interview she inquired whether it was interesting enough – a concern not likely to be shared by a front-office banker. She need not have worried.

She had worked for two megabanks and no matter how different their cultures were, it came down the same question for both: 'Can you blame a CEO for a scandal at his bank? Given the size of banks, all a CEO can be guilty of is delegating to the wrong person. How can you possibly have oversight of 100,000 employees?' Her bank processed millions of transactions 24 hours a day, every day of the week, around the world. It had gigantic portfolios with loans and was involved in activities of a widely different and varying nature and complexity. The question is not only how much risk you are running as a bank, she said. The question is if you even know what you own at any given point. 'You have got the trader, who passes the information about his trades on to a "product controller", who passes it on to the finance team in the investment banking operation, who then pass it on to us. That's a lot of layers.'

At her megabank there was both a commercial and an investment banking division. Here, too, there were many layers since she did not deal with actual investment bankers but rather with their finance team. So they are accountants rather than bankers, she explained, adding that the investment bank's finance team is 'far more secretive, displaying a "you don't need to know" attitude and making us feel as if it's them who are in charge. They seem to want to drive the agenda and to control the way their department is portrayed. In most companies, group financial reporting sits above all finance teams working in that company,' she continued. 'But in some banks where the investment arm makes most of the group's profits, it's more as if we're this sideshow for them. People in my team can feel too intimated to properly query the numbers, they feel like "it's not my place to ask." Before the crisis of 2008 we had very little insight into the numbers in the investment bank.'

A lot has changed since then, she emphasised, and she now felt 'definitely more empowered' to ask tough questions. Still, the problem remains that 'nobody really understands the banks any more, and that includes insiders. Every season we do the same thing, to a set timetable, leading to the same results that allow the bank to say: look, it's under control. We are meant to understand the bank, and show the numbers illustrating that understanding. In reality it's almost the other way around, we have a process in place to collect the numbers and if that collection takes place properly and every step is followed, then the outcome is recognised as legitimate. It's a legitimising operation.'

In his memoirs *Back from the Brink*, former Labour chancellor Alistair Darling remarks drily that one hears a lot about financial institution that are 'too big to fail' and possibly even 'too big to save.' There is, however, another category, writes the man who had to 'save' a number of British banks during the crash: institutions that are 'too big to know what's going on.'

'Too big to manage' is the phrase insiders use and the least understood but most important aspect of this seems to be IT. Remember that banks did not grow slowly and organically to their current size, said people working with banks' IT systems. They grew in jumps, so to speak, by taking over or merging with other banks and financial institutions of wildly varying size and complexity, spread out over the globe. Meanwhile, funding for IT systems is often inadequate – if only because such long-term investments come at the expense of short-term profits. In many banks, the front, middle and back office have different systems, and one bank has different systems in different countries. These systems have evolved over the years, step by step, one added to another. IT specialists talked about 'patches' for new products that need to be integrated into these myriad systems, and about 'work-arounds': improvised solutions when an activity or product cannot be properly processed. There are systems in order to run all these systems, systems to run those and so on.

'Your readers would be shocked if they realised just how crap the IT organisation is in many banks as well as corporations and government ministries,' said a man with a decade of experience in a software company. 'Sometimes we get a glimpse, when a company is unavailable for days due to "computer problems." Have you noticed these cases always take longer than expected? This is not because repairs take long. Finding out what the problem is in the first place – "root cause analysis" – that's nearly always the most time-consuming. Nobody has a complete and in-depth overview.'

He seemed genuinely concerned that one day a megabank would be shut out of its own data. What happens to the companies who rely on that bank's payment system? 'It would make the panic during a bank run look innocent.' He spoke of colleagues who retain paper copies of all their internet banking statements and confirmed with a grin a favourite quote of mine from another IT specialist I'd interviewed: 'The generation who built the computer systems when automation took off is now reaching retirement age. So there we are, called into a bank to solve a problem. They take us to a greying man sitting in the corner: "Please meet Peter, he is the only one left around here who still understands the systems."'

IT people are prone to exaggeration, said many non-IT banking staff, but both groups agreed that the wobbliness and opacity of systems make the big banks fundamentally vulnerable. 'You'd expect banks to have these super systems where you simply press a button and out comes what you need,' said a compliance officer. 'In reality I have to do a lot of "manual reconstruction." Say I need to see what a client of our bank has been up to, what kind of trades he has done. It's surprisingly difficult to get that information. I'd have to go myself into several systems, lift out bits here and there, then assemble a picture.'

One consultant even said: 'The next global financial blow-up will begin with an IT crash.'

•

It was hard work, finding answers to the question of whether investment and megabanks in their current form are still manageable. But as the interviews piled up, the inevitable logic behind yet another scandal began to become clear. Early into the life of the blog, the Swiss bank UBS was forced to acknowledge that one its traders, Kweku Adoboli, had lost $2 billion. Contrary to the London Whale, Adoboli had broken lots of rules and laws, making him a so-called 'rogue trader.' Every few years a scandal of this kind breaks out, the best-known examples being British trader Nick Leeson who in 1995 singlehandedly brought down the centuries-old British bank Barings, and French trader Jérôme Kerviel who in 2008 managed to lose €4.9 billion for Société Générale. In court, the prosecution portrayed Adoboli as a selfish man craving status and ever-bigger bonuses. This was the familiar trope of finance as a casino for greedy monsters. However, banking staff and financial professionals had far more interesting things to say.

'We are seen as boring people,' said a consultant who helped banks prevent and detect rogue trading. 'The truth is that to do my job well, Ihave to be a really cynical Sherlock Holmes.' Her firm employed former police officers to help with interrogations techniques, IT specialists for the systems and financial experts to understand the products. She was in charge of one of those teams. 'It's a great job as it's project-based. We go somewhere, solve a problem and leave again, onto the next project.' She felt no need to defend rogue traders, she emphasised, but remember that trading floors can be extremely masculine environments. 'It's like a playground full of boys. They egg each other on. So here's this trader and he takes a risk in a trade and he loses. He can't admit this to himself, to his mates, to his superior. So he covers it up with a new risky trade, which goes wrong again.' At this point the alarm bells in internal controls are meant to go off but a rogue trader will know the vast computer systems inside out – perhaps because he started out in the back office himself. So he manages to hide his losses for now, thinking he will be able to recoup them soon, cover up his tracks and all will be well. This works, sometimes, but every now and then the losses accumulate to a point when it becomes impossible to conceal them any longer.

This is why the Holmes-like consultant always focused on the culture in a bank. 'Is this a place where somebody can raise his hand and say I made a mistake? Does that get you a round of applause, or a round of sniggering? I know banks where admitting you got something wrong is not a smart thing to do.'

Other interviewees who dealt directly with the issue said the same thing: rogue trading is not about greed. It is about despair and it is a direct consequence of how the banks are now organised. They also said: there is a lot more going on that you won't hear about in the news.

An operational risk officer whose task was to verify traders' profit and loss accounts talked about a leak that his bank had fixed only recently – and still not entirely: 'Every trader runs one or more so-called "books" with all his trades. But when a trader leaves for another job, the book usually stays on the system. So you have thousands of old books from traders who stopped years ago. Somebody with intimate knowledge of the systems might try to squirrel away some trades. Truth is that the scale and complexity of a major bank's trading operation makes for opportunities.'

•

From the elite university pedigrees and superbly designed logos and websites to the job titles and the confident attitude on the part of top bankers when facing questions from the media or parliamentary committees, banks are very good at creating the impression of being run like an army or an airport. You assume they are structured around efficient hierarchies with a steady flow of commands, information and feedback between top and base. But look beyond the facade at the perverse incentives, at the silos and the climate of fear, at how zero job security breeds zero loyalty and at their unmanageable size and complexity and you do not see a rationally organised command structure. You see a cluster of islands in the fog, staffed by mercenaries.

An environment like this offers immense temptations. When somebody takes advantage of these opportunities, is that an unfortunate incident brought about by a rotten apple or rather a symptom of a deeper problem? Proof that megabanks in their current form are simply dysfunctional?

Then – finally – I found someone who in 2008 had been really close to the action.

8

And Now for Some Good News?

While doing research there are sometimes points at which lines of investigation suddenly coalesce into an insight. One such moment occurred during a very long conversation with a banker who had worked at two prestigious investment banks around the time of the crash, on trading floors that built and sold collateralised debt obligations (CDOs) – the kind of products that blew up in 2008.

The CDO banker was in his forties, gentle and self-deprecating, describing himself with a note of pride as a 'university drop-out who ended up in banking by luck and found out that I really enjoy it and I am quite good at it. I'd do it for far less, too.'

Born and raised on the continent, he had worked there for a while in private banking, investing and managing rich people's money. Around the turn of the millennium, a megabank had brought him over to London to sell financial products to these well-to-do clients.

At his suggestion we met in the hotel where 15 years earlier his bank had put him up as they completed his recruitment process. He had never been back and looked around almost with nostalgia. What would he tell his younger self? 'I don't know . . . enjoy it?'

He pointed to the luxury surrounding us. 'Before you sign on, investment banks treat you like a star. Then your job starts and you're one of many.' He vividly remembered the first time he got onto the trading floor. It was a world away from the 'client-facing' side of investment banks where it is all 'expensive suits, excellent catering, antiques on the walls.' On trading floors, hundreds and hundreds of people sit in front of screens. 'Factories. You've got a computer, phone and Bloomberg terminal with financial data and that's it.' He realised: this is the heart of the machine.

His bank had an in-house dentist, a doctor, a dry-cleaning service, a travel agent, restaurants, and fitness facilities – everything to make you as productive and focused on making money as possible. His trading floor had a food trolley so there was no need to leave your desk when you got hungry. There was even a guy going around the trading floor polishing your shoes for a few pounds.

The CDO banker stirred his tea, and broke the short silence with a joke: 'Where does an 800lb gorilla sit? Wherever he wants to. A newcomer is the opposite of an 800lb gorilla. You have to fight your way in. Nobody has time. Nobody cares who you are. But you have been brought in with a budget. This is the money you have to make for the bank or out you go.'

His bank would sometimes hire two people for the same role and see who survived. He had been promised a 'client segment' all to himself, only to discover on his first day that, actually, several others already worked on that area of the market. 'Basically I was not allowed to call anyone in that segment.' Even worse: the manager who had hired him had left for another bank almost as soon as he started, so he was left to fend for himself.

He remembered taking a very deep breath and saying to himself, 'OK, this is going to be harder than I thought.' Over time, he'd learn that success in an investment bank is down to defining, claiming and defending your territory – both in terms of the kind of products you are licensed by the bank to sell to clients and your geographical area. Back then, all he realised was that he had to do something noticeable to stake his claim.

Before coming to London he had known next to nothing about CDOs. He had been hired purely for his reputation for good relationships with clients who trusted him when he worked as a private banker. But he had a good head for maths, read up as fast as he could and after a while an idea came to him. He knew that one client's portfolio of investments was exposed to a particular risk. Could a so-called 'hybrid synthetic CDO' offer protection? To find out he would have to ask a structurer, someone who designs and builds complex instruments and does the calculations behind it. 'Now, it's not like you can just go up to these guys,' he explained. 'Everybody is extremely busy, all the time. I remember when on one of the TV screens, there was a silly Bloomberg item about the latest *Sports Illustrated* swimsuit issue. I didn't mind looking at pictures of beautiful ladies but nobody around me was taking any notice. They were all just glued to their computer screens.'

He arranged for an expensive sandwich to be delivered to the desk of one of the structurers. Next he went up to him and said, while you eat that, let me tell you about this idea. Perhaps the structurer thought that was ballsy but in any case, he listened. Then the structurer asked: who is it for? 'And of course I gave an evasive answer because someone else on the floor may know that client too and try to steal the idea from me.'

His idea worked. The client liked it and suddenly he was this new guy who had done a $2 million deal. He did more deals until another bank approached him. Again he was promised the whole of the country he was specialised in. Again many others turned out to be working on that same segment. 'I suppose I am a slow learner,' he said with a laugh.

At his new bank he had to fight his way in all over again but this time he knew the rules of the game, and what he was up against: thousands of bankers working in their own individual segments all trying to do the same thing – invent solutions for clients. 'So you need to know as much as possible about your clients' needs. Your products must compete with other banks. Meanwhile at the back of your mind you think: I have to hit my profit and loss number or there's no bonus and basically redundancy.'

To set yourself apart in this universe, he discovered, you need to be the first to come up with a new product – and make the most of it while the margins are still fat. 'You know that soon enough other banks will offer the same product. Margins come down, things get standardised and commoditised. How do other banks catch on? They copy your product. Or they poach some of your colleagues to set up a desk. Or they poach you.'

Think of an investment bank as a bunch of franchises, he said. 'There's very limited middle management or anything like that. It's a huge machinery for executing transactions and deals but you're effectively on your own to make those happen. Everybody – and I mean everybody is focused on business, on "revenue responsibility."' At the same time everything in the two investment banks he worked for was 'up for grabs.' Claiming deals and making sure you get 'production credits' for contributing is an endless preoccupation.

His former boss's job title was the 'head of western Europe.' Even he had to bring in revenue, in his case between 10 and 20 million a year. 'How much time do you think he had for managing? He knew he'd be in trouble if he didn't make his budget.'

A waiter brought us sandwiches. The CDO banker continued explaining how many of the products built and sold on his trading floor would run over many years, much like mortgages or insurance plans. The thing is, he said, your share in the expected profits on the product is booked on your bonus of that year. 'Obviously if you can book the future revenue of the next seven years in one go, that's a huge number. This is one of the reasons why bonuses shot up the way they did.'

He had seen with his own eyes how this reward system could make people 'aggressive. 'Say this year you got a huge bonus. How about next year? That's right, you need to keep selling these products, year in year out. This was one factor driving innovation and the development of ever more complex products.' Given these incentives, your attitude towards your clients can change, too. 'You don't need to maintain a relationship over many years. Sell a client one product and bang, you're there.'

He knew of colleagues who had become financially independent very quickly on the back of this reward system. 'First they did a few huge deals, next they let another bank recruit them for a huge guaranteed bonus. The thinking at the new bank was: if this guy can make £15 million in a year we can pay him a few million.'

Meanwhile the clients his trading floor catered to were 'professional investors,' meaning caveat emptor applied. Many were able to understand what they were buying, he said, but not everyone. 'I could tell you stories about the German Landesbanken.'

Still, he said repeatedly during the interview, most of his colleagues were decent people. 'Some said about CDOs, no way, I'm just not getting into any of that. But CDOs are neutral instruments. If you fill them with toxic assets, of course it's going to get ugly. All my CDOs have paid out.'

•

Until I met the CDO banker I had assumed that you could not understand the crash without first understanding how CDOs and their 'ever more complex varieties' exactly worked. So I had diligently thrown myself into the literature and slowly grasped that you can use CDOs to spread the risk of default on a 'pool' of loans. A CDO 'squared' is a CDO containing other CDOs while in a 'synthetic' CDO you do not actually own any of the underlying loans but agree to pay another party when the loans go up in value – or vice versa. A 'hybrid' CDO can consist of both 'synthetic' and regular CDOs.

Weed out the jargon, simplify radically and boil everything down to its essence and the working of CDOs and their 'ever more complex varieties' becomes broadly comprehensible.

But as I was listening to the CDO banker I began to wonder: how relevant is all this anyway? The issue is not whether outsiders can be made to understand how these complex products worked but rather why, before the crash, so few insiders took an interest.

The answer to that question can be found in the CDO banker's story: vast trading floors where mercenaries survive in a haze of complexity and caveat emptor; an atmosphere of deep mutual distrust; a relentless and amoral focus on profit and 'revenue responsibility'; a brutal hire and fire culture . . . Why would people on a trading floor worry about the risks or ethics of the complex financial products they were selling, let alone about the long-term financial health of their own bank? Why would they even think about it as 'their' bank, knowing they could be out of the door in five minutes – either fired without prior warning or poached by a competitor? Why would a risk manager or compliance officer in such an environment sound the alarm? Why not screw your client given that it is all perfectly legal and you are under immense pressure to 'perform'?

This was beginning to look almost like a blueprint for short-termism.

I managed to interview a few of the most senior people in banking – board members and a CEO, for example — but their quotes were usually too distinctive for me to be able to keep them anonymous. However, reports published since the crash corroborate the suggestion that at least in some banks the short-termist mindset described by the CDO banker ran all the way to the top, certainly in the years before 2008. In his memoirs, Alistair Darling writes about the top bankers he had to negotiate bailouts with in the dark days of the crash:

> They didn't understand what they were doing, the risks they were taking on, or, often, the products they were selling. At the height of the crisis, one leading banker told me with pride that his bank had just decided they would no longer take any risk they didn't understand. I think that was supposed to reassure me. It didn't; it horrified me. The top management in banks both here and in the US failed to understand – or even ask – what was apparently making them so much profit and what were the risks.

'They had failed to understand or even ask.' Of all the reasons to stop calling investment banks casinos, this must be the most important. Playing roulette, you know the odds: a little under 50 per cent for red and black and one in 37 for the numbers.

In investment banking the rampant complexity makes

many risks extremely difficult to measure. Things are ambiguous, obfuscated and often deliberately opaque – 'intransparent' is the word used by insiders. A new product can turn a profit – or not. How are you to know, as risk manager, head of western Europe or CEO? Meanwhile, banks selling these products and taking other lucrative risks make huge short-term profits and will see themselves celebrated by shareholders and the financial media. In a probably inadvertent moment of candour the highest boss of the megabank Citigroup summarised this dynamic as: 'As long as the music is playing, you've got to get up and dance.' He then added: 'We're still dancing.' That was July 2007.

At this point, it would be nice to present some good news. A book needs that, 60 per cent into the story. Time for a breather, to recover from all the bad stuff, and definitely time to give the reader a 'good' protagonist, someone who is fighting the good fight on our behalf.

I certainly needed that. Longing for something positive, I focused on the institutions that are meant to be a check on the banks. Why did credit rating agencies assign triple-A or 'super-safe' ratings to so many CDOs and their ever more complex varieties? Why had the external accountants tasked with auditing the banks' books failed to see or say anything? Where were the regulators in all this?

The search for answers seemed promising when an email by one William J Harrington arrived. We arranged to meet for an interview. A large, well-dressed American in his forties, Harrington was very proud of his New England background. He had worked for over 10 years at the credit rating agency Moody's, in the division that assigned triple-A ratings to CDOs filled with mortgages. Harrington had left without a severance package and was waging what he described as a one-man guerrilla war against Moody's and other credit rating agencies. His weapon: publicity. He had no objections to me using his full name. Finally I could give some colour and background to an interviewee.

After training as an economist, Harrington had gone to work for the investment bank Merrill Lynch. People there always seemed to want more, more, more, he said, adding: 'The reward system is just so . . . straight. You see people get old before their time because their primary concern seems to be finding the next deal. They seem to lose everything that makes them unique. And they have this enormous sense of self-importance.'

He knew rating agencies were seen as losers and also-rans but didn't care. He didn't go to conferences or industry parties anyway. Cross-industry surveys put Moody's at the top of good places to work for gay people so, partly for that reason, he applied.

People would sometimes ask of Moody's: 'Why is it so gay here?' he said. I told him that in the City the regulators have a similar image and Harrington nodded: 'I suppose that once a place establishes itself as gay-friendly, others will gravitate towards it.' Then his smile faded: 'I suspect some of the most toxic managers at Moody's liked to hire beaten-up people who may have felt they had few options – making people feel indebted because they aren't being homophobic.'

Waging a one-man 'guerrilla' campaign against a powerful institution such as Moody's invites powerful responses, not all of them positive. Throughout the interview Harrington seemed tense. He spoke of his former employer almost like a son deeply disappointed by his father. Increasingly, the bankers drove the rating process, he said. 'In my days it was individual managers who set the rules of how to interact with the bankers,' he explained, 'for instance whether we could scream back at them.' He paused for effect and added: 'We could not.'

Bang. This was one of those statements that was as telling and potentially explosive as it was impossible to verify. The same goes for his comment about 'toxic managers' deliberately hiring gays for their presumed vulnerability and Harrington's judgment that by 2006 the environment at Moody's had also turned 'toxic.' Moody's themselves have refused to comment on Harrington's claims. However, when it came to the business model of the big credit rating agencies anyone can check Harrington's reports for themselves. It is true, for example, that credit rating agencies are paid by the very banks whose complex financial products and instruments they are meant to judge independently. It is also the case that Moody's and similar agencies argued that their ratings were merely 'opinions,' or free speech, and they have never been held accountable for their triple-A surfeit. Harrington noted drily: 'The CEO of Moody's in the run-up to the fiasco in 2008 is now . . . still the CEO of Moody's. Last year his compensation was $6 million, in line with his five-year average. Rating agencies make so much money.'

All of this is verifiable, as is the fact that only three agencies control 95 per cent of the market for credit ratings. Harrington needed few words to explain why an 'oligopoly' of this kind causes the free market to stop functioning: 'If there were many significant rating agencies of varying sizes and ownership structures (rather than three indistinguishable large ones) and a few changed their approach, it would be hard for the rest to simply continue to go along for the ride. Currently, this is not a self-correcting system.'

The reason all of this has stayed with me, I think, is that for the first time I was feeling something very close to real anger.

This could not be true, could it? Imagine the Michelin-guide inspectors getting paid by the chef whose food they had come to taste? How many stars would that restaurant get?

There was more. An external accountant of around 30 years old said that during an audit of a bank – 'the client,' in his words – you need to 'find stuff that we can take into the meeting with the client, so we can say, look, this is what we found, can you explain that? How do we justify our fee if we dig up absolutely nothing?' But there is a flipside. 'The more we find, the more extra work we need to do. That pushes up our cost to the client, or eats into our revenues. You could argue that on an individual basis accountants are incentivised not to find something.'

That was just one voice. But there is no way of avoiding the fact that the world of City accounting, like that of ratings agencies, is dominated by a handful of firms: KPMG, Ernst & Young, Deloitte and PwC. They even have a nickname: the Big Four. In the past decades banks have hardly ever, if at all, switched accountants and even more interesting: not only do the Big Four audit the big banks' books, they also have immense consultancy arms selling highly priced advice to . . . those same banks! To go back to the analogy of the restaurant, the auditor is acting like a health and safety inspector who not only rates the kitchen hygiene but also makes big sums on the side advising the cook how to increase revenue.

Perhaps this state of things explains why in two years I did not meet a single banker or banking staff member who spoke respectfully about external accountants. Consider for example the internal accountant in group financial reporting who called her own work a 'legitimising operation.' Of external auditors she said, almost indignantly: 'How can they make independent judgments of us when we are their biggest clients? You show external auditors a piece of paper with the number on it that they're looking for and they go: OK. I mean, to know what that number corresponds to you'd have to see evidence, you'd need to have a breakdown of how the business unit operates. Given how unintrusive external auditors are we could have a whole separate accounting system without them knowing.'

•

Over at the *Guardian* we decided to 'offer fate a bit of a helping hand,' as we say in Holland. A trader had asked, rhetorically, in his interview: 'Do we, as a society, want 25-year-old traders making £1 million a year? If not, you need regulation, on a global scale. The trouble is, regulators are idiots. I am sorry to put it so bluntly but you can't expect it any other way. Why would a smart, aggressive, competitive 22-year-old decide to work for the regulators?'

It helped that when we put the piece online we used 'The trouble is, regulators are idiots' as the headline. Twenty-four hours later, two regulators had come forward: one junior and one senior. Finally.

The junior regulator had read economics at an elite university and most of his peers had gone into banking. Their starting salary was £45,000 plus bonus. After receiving a one-off signing bonus of £2,500, the junior regulator had started with a little under £30,000. 'I actually have a life,' he said, by way of explanation as to his career choice. 'I get my weekends.' And the work he did – 'consumer protection, aiming to make the financial sector more stable' – had a higher purpose than chasing a profit margin.

I attempted my usual ice-breaker of asking what kind of animal he was and with a hint of irritation he began to think out loud: 'There are not too many of us, but we're very big. We never forget. We're very powerful, though we can be somewhat clumsy. We're not predators but, when you hear us coming, you pay attention . . . I suppose the elephants.'

The regulators attract very bright people from the top universities, he insisted, referring to the trader's 'idiots' comment. What's more, he continued: 'Banks have been so wrong about their risks. There was a clamour for light-touch regulation, to leave the industry in peace, because they knew best. People blame the regulators for missing all sorts of things in years past, and there were regulatory failures. But the senior management and risk people inside the banks should have caught them in the first place. Then again, those risk officers who did issue warnings in those years may have been let go.'

Since the crash, the regulators were 'losing people at all levels,' he said. Recently there had been a string of morale-sapping high-profile departures to 'the other side' – as regulators sometimes call the banks. 'You start thinking, "If the bosses are all jumping ship, where does that leave me?" The financial industry is hiring for positions requiring exactly the skills we have – compliance and risk management. I do wonder at what point I would stop saying no. When the time comes to have kids? London is expensive. Some difficult life choices lie ahead.'

Heading for the tube we walked past Abacus, a place where young women go to 'bag a banker,' I suggested he go there and he laughed: 'Well, my girlfriend would bust my balls.'

Later that afternoon an email comes in: 'Another thought: the girls in Abacus aren't as impressed by my business card! Regulation may have a higher purpose but it's not sexy!'

The junior regulator had been at university during the crash. But the senior regulator had been right in the thick of it. With more than my usual curiosity I headed to Canary Wharf where we were meeting some distance from the regulator's offices. He was a relaxed-looking and soft-spoken man of around 35 who described his politics as 'centre-left.' He listened calmly to my questions and took his time to answer.

Comments about bankers as 'money-grabbing bastards' are off the mark, he thought. 'It's not the people who are bad: it's the culture that builds up all these material expectations. People come in, they see that the successful people are the arseholes, and they imitate this kind of bigoted, mouthy person in the hope of getting ahead themselves.'

His career had started in a big investment bank and while he did not want to 'blow his own trumpet,' as he put it, his performance reviews always said that he 'exceeded expectations.' Still, he felt an increasing ambivalence over the nature of his work, which had gradually grown into disillusionment. His friends from university were all teachers, doctors, police officers. He now believes that the public-sector background of his social circle helped keep him grounded. Also, 'I just wasn't into luxury goods.'

Once he knew that he did not want to stay in banking, he thought: where can I use my skills usefully? Answer: at the regulator. Lots of his colleagues came from banks. You need a mix, he explained: 'Outsiders whose fresh perspective allows them to ask the simple big questions, and former insiders like me who can cut through the bullshit that banks feed you.'

There are around a million people working in finance in the UK today, he estimated. The regulator has around 5,000 people. 'Not exactly man-to-man marking, is it? The banks will always have more resources.'

The regulator deploys teams to every major bank to do what is essentially 'policing work,' he said. 'Close and continuous supervision' was the term now in vogue. 'We have regular meetings with senior management, usually the managing directors – most people in the industry won't have any contact with us. The goal is to understand the risks they're undertaking. You identify an area of concern, then drill down to the granular level. The key is to see whether they themselves understand their risks, then make sure they're addressing them. In the past it was too easy to regard the banks . . . maybe not as our clients, but there was a degree of regulatory capture. These days it's a lot less cosy.'

So how did that work before 2008 with the CDOs and their ever more complex varieties? 'Most of the time the sales people have no idea what they're selling,' he said. Those who invented and built the products did, of course. 'They got it past their internal risk and compliance people by presenting them with a sanitised version, rounding off the risky edges and making it seem simpler and safer. Then these risk and compliance people present it to us.'

Ultimately, regulators rely on self-declaration: what is presented by a bank's internal management. The trouble is, he said with a perfectly calm smile, a bank's internal management often don't know what's going on themselves because banks today are so vast and hugely complex.

He did not think he had ever been deliberately lied to, though he acknowledged that, obviously, he couldn't know this for sure. 'The real threat is not a bank's management hiding things from us: it's the management not knowing themselves what the risks are, either because nobody realises it or because some people are keeping it from their bosses.'

He talked about the culture of fear and how people are not managing their actions for the benefit of their bank. Instead, 'they are managing their career. If you are regarded as a "golden boy", the crucial thing is not to drop the ball. You're in the slipstream up towards the top, and the last thing you want to do is commit yourself to risky decisions.'

This is why he believed that the crash had been more 'cock-up than conspiracy.' Bank management is in conflict, he pointed out. 'What is good for the long term of the bank or the country may not be what is best for their own short-term career or bonus.'

I brought up the quote about regulators being idiots and he just shrugged if off. 'The perception is that the regulator is sort of the B-team, those who didn't make it in, or into, the banks. It really doesn't seem like that at all, on the ground. There is more room to be eccentric here, certainly, as the culture is less conformist. But B-team? Just ask recruiters – they give us job offers at banks all the time.'

And it's not as if you would need to apply, he went on. 'Recruiters get hold of your CV and make offers on behalf of banks. It's easy to understand why. I know exactly how the regulators work and what they want banks to do. I know precisely how bad it needs to get for a bank to be referred for enforcement, and then I know exactly what happens in that case.'

Now his face tensed up slightly, only to break into a new affable smile: 'There's no one at the regulator who couldn't make 30 or 40 per cent more working for a bank. As I said, I used to work for one. If I had stayed, given the path I was on, my pay would be two or three times more than what I am on now.'

By taking this job, he had definitely turned away from the lifestyle he was heading towards. 'That's the true test of character, if you can say no to earning three, four or five times your current salary.'

•

I could still sketch out in great detail the sunlit corner of Canary Wharf we were sitting – on a bench in the shade opposite a coffee kiosk. I remember vividly, too, how on taking the Docklands Light Railway back to the *Guardian* offices the sunlight reflected in the glass towers made my eyes squint.

It was like that meeting with Harrington earlier. Then I

had felt anger for the first time. Now a form of despair and real fear began to come over me. I suppose that until meeting that senior regulator I had a sliver of hope of hearing some good news, and a convincing reason that everything had been done to avoid a repeat of the last crash. 'Has the sector been fixed after the crisis?' I asked him straight out. His answer: 'I don't think so.' The denial phase was coming to an end.

9

Godverdomme

There does not seem to have been any systematic polling on this, but my impression is that very few people outside finance are even aware that in 2008, life as we know it had a near-death experience.

This makes sense. Nobody who saw the threat had an interest in increasing the panic by talking about it. The almost supernaturally level-headed former president of the European Council, Herman van Rompuy, waited until 2014 to acknowledge in an interview that six years earlier we had been within 'a few millimetres from a total implosion.'

It is also much easier to make a Hollywood blockbuster about the threat posed by asteroids, pandemics or an alien invasion than about something as abstract as the global financial system in its current form. Equally unhelpful is the code of silence smothering or distorting signals coming from inside the sector, and the fact that in school you hardly learn a thing about the theory and practice of the financial system. I don't think I'm alone in having been taught more about the ancient Egyptians than about the banks or our system of money creation.

The general ignorance about the current threat posed by the financial system came across very clearly every time anyone asked me at parties, over dinner or at the school gates what had surprised me most about 'those bankers.' The question often came with a cynical laugh as if nothing genuinely serious was at stake; they seemed to anticipate my answer would be 'greed,' 'cocaine' or 'arrogance.' Many referred to the Gordon Gekko character from the iconic 1987 film *Wall Street* and his famous quote: 'Greed, for want of a better word, is good.'

I would resist pointing out that Gordon Gekko was not a banker but a 'corporate raider' or 'activist shareholder' taking over companies against their will, and instead I'd tell them how some of the things I'd learnt about bankers had 'lightning-bolted me off my horse,' as the Flemish expression goes.

I had had no idea just how much damage the financial sector can do to society let alone how terrifying close to the brink we were in 2008. However, what had struck me even more is how such organisations continue to be governed by a system of incentives that seem almost designed to encourage short-termism. Imagine people telling you without any anxiety, let alone shame, that their bank is just a 'replaceable' platform or a shell. As one trader with a smaller bank in the City had put it: 'You need a place to trade from, this is how we saw our bank. An entire team can be poached and go from one bank to another. There's no loyalty either way. And the top at your bank has no idea what's going on – how could they? Why would anyone tell them what's going on?'

It's a dog eat dog world, the trader would continue: every man for himself and all of us against the bank. 'Even the head of markets, the guy in charge of all the traders, was on the side of the traders, against the bank. Management consists of traders who have worked their way up. What kind of people do you think they are?'

This was not the answer people expected and many became visibly uncomfortable as they absorbed it. Several inquired whether perhaps my interviewees were exaggerating – had I been taken in by their over-dramatisation or personal grievances disguised as revelations?

For a long time, this is exactly what I, too, had been wondering, even hoping. Who wants to live in a world where problems of this magnitude are not even public knowledge, let alone in the process of being solved? For an impressive period of time I had managed to stay in denial and I remember exactly when that phase came to an end and reality broke through – like a seawall finally breached by the pounding of waves.

The first wave hit at a press conference. The *Guardian* had sent me to cover the annual results announcement of three British 'too big to fail' banks in March 2013. This was something of a contrast to all my clandestine meetings. Suddenly I found myself invited into giant shiny buildings with imposing views of London. There were around 20 journalists and our allotted role seemed to be to sit there while the CEO buried us in numbers, percentages, ratios and pie charts. In a tone suggesting many years of experience with press conferences of this kind, the CEO would say things like: 'We remain very confident of our capital position,' and 'Our strategy remains centred on taking into account the interests of all of our stakeholders.' Potential fines for the recent scandals were referred to as 'legacy issues' requiring 'customer redress,' while HSBC politely referred to a monster fine of $1.9 billion for drug money laundering imposed by the U.S. authorities as 'regulatory and law enforcement matters.'

The weekend before the conferences began we had been handed the annual results reports. Excluding the appendices, the one for RBS came to 289 pages, HSBC's was 550 pages and Lloyds' was 165.

During the conference we were allowed to ask questions. 'What was that £250 million for?' asked one journalist. How was the CEO's pay structured, asked another, and when did the CEOs think that RBS and Lloyds would return into private hands so we could see if 'taxpayers will get their money back'?

The CEOs addressed most journalists by their first names, and then gave long and meaningless answers. When it was over there were tasty sandwiches and fruit while the journalist next to me remarked: 'Until recently I did political news. The peculiar thing is that theoretically you can survive in financial journalism without actually knowing what is going on. There are always new numbers and results coming out. You collect a few reactions to those and off you go to the next wave of numbers and results.'

The two banks dependent on the government funding made their CEO and board members available for informal chats before and after the press conference while HSBC, which isn't, made do with an early-morning telephone conference call to selected journalists during which almost half of the time was taken up by the head of the bank reading out a prepared text.

The Lloyds and RBS press conferences were strikingly similar and after a weekend of turning those spectacles over in my mind it finally dawned on me: I had witnessed a ritual. The flood of numbers and PR phrases, the focus among journalists on bonuses and relatively innocent details . . . Consciously or unconsciously, the press, together with those CEOs, had been staging a performance that sent the subliminal message: it is back to business as usual. Yes, banks have tens and tens of thousands of employees, often spread out over many countries and engaged in very different and often deeply opaque activities across the globe. Yes, over the past half-decade or so those banks have been caught out by scandal after scandal somewhere in their vast empires, and yes, in the past their books gave a wildly inaccurate if not deliberately misleading picture of the risks they were running.

But all of this was now in the past and firmly under control, the CEOs implied, and with a start it hit me: as an average citizen or reader I would have fallen for this, happily thinking that the financial system is safe again and now all we need to do is sort out those bonuses – because that is the issue that politicians and the media focus on. But my ignorance phase was over, and I'd moved beyond denial. This time, I felt pure anger.

When I made a brief trip back to the Netherlands, I realised I had to try and see an old friend, Peter van Ees. We grew up in the same neighbourhood in a suburb to the south of Amsterdam. In our youth we had played defence together, not entirely convincingly, for our local football team. After practice we would cycle home, two nerds chewing over the pros and cons of choosing Latin over Greek and vice versa.

We may not have seen as much of each other over the last two decades but the bond ran deep. Peter grew up to be a very successful investment banker at the Amsterdam office of the Swiss bank UBS. I knew that even though he had recently switched jobs he'd be able to talk knowledgeably about high finance and investment banking and when we sat down in Café Americain on the Leidseplein in Amsterdam my first question was about the code of silence. As a former Netherlands-based investment banker, Peter felt there was no reason not to speak openly about the sector, provided he maintained the usual confidentiality towards the bank and its clients. Thirty-five years after playing together at FC Actif, there we were, two boys playing grown-up in Amsterdam's poshest grand café.

Interviewing people is a strange thing to do. You meet someone for the first time and in a very intensive and often peculiarly intimate atmosphere you try to harvest as much information and insight as you can. You continue by email or telephone to finesse the text and then you never see each other again. I stayed in touch with a few interviewees but most were one-off meetings, and perhaps this is why their stories about the global financial system and the City's central role in it had somehow remained abstract for me, as if it only affected or threatened others. Until I sat there sipping expensive coffee and eating toasted sandwiches with Peter.

Going this far back with someone meant we could skip the small talk and have a truly honest conversation with trust on both sides. This was why I had been so keen to see Peter. I felt almost reluctant to press for the truth. Were the interviewees' stories about the hours and days following the collapse of Lehman Brothers really true? The hoarding of food, cash and gold, the preparations for the evacuation of the children to the countryside, the alleged stockpiling of arms . . . If there was anyone who could give me a convincing answer it was Peter. He would set me straight if these anecdotes were crazy exaggerations. Even by Dutch standards he was extremely level-headed.

'I remember looking out of the window and seeing the buses drive by,' Peter said. 'People everywhere going through a normal working day. Or so they thought. They have no idea, I realised. I did. My colleagues did, too. For the first time in my life I called my father from the office to tell him to transfer all his savings to a safer bank. Which he promptly did. When I went home that day I was genuinely terrified. I thought: so this is what the threat of war must feel like.'

•

Godverdomme. If you'd have to capture my mood after the meeting with Peter this Dutch version of 'fucking hell' comes closest. All of this has really happened. And far worse: it could very well happen again.

So many interviewees had said the same thing: 'it is business as usual again.' Since 2008 there has been a relentless flood of pious platitudes about 'lessons learnt' and 'the need to regain the public's trust.' The parliamentary commissions into the crash dug laboriously into the causes and resulted in a raft of new rules and regulations that were designed to avoid it happening again. The middle office now has slightly more power and status, it has become more expensive for big banks to be big, and many high up in the front office have gone on costly 'culture change' courses. But the underlying perverse incentives in the financial sector have been left mostly unchanged.

Banks must now hold higher capital buffers, or rather they must finance a larger part of their risks with equity rather than borrowed money. The buffers are still much lower than for most of financial history and while they are meant to go up further still, this restriction won't be in place for years.

American banks are now banned from using their own capital to speculate and invest in the markets ('prop trading'), more or less, and the European Commission has forced a few banks to shrink or sell their investment bank activities – with the unintended consequence of making it even easier for the remaining banks to divide up markets among themselves since there are no new banks joining the fray.

Though some have shrunk or dismantled their investment divisions, the banks have not been chopped up into units that are simple and small enough to safely fail. Instead, if a bank collapses, the European Banking Union is meant to step in and wind it down in an orderly fashion. Who is behind that European Banking Union should a real panic cause many banks to fail at the same time? That's right: the taxpayer.

The de facto cartels and niches where a handful of banks make monster profits by cornering the market continue as before. The European Union has imposed a bonus cap but this has simply led the banks to raise the fixed salaries and lower the bonuses – effectively obscuring the monster profits from view.

The list of measures taken is longer but the underlying pattern remains the same: the regulatory response to the crash of 2008 has been to fight the symptoms instead of the cause. Instead of a fresh start with clear and simple laws there are endless new rules. Now it is even harder to set up a new bank because those rules require huge numbers of expensive risk and compliance staff and how is a new bank going to find the money to pay those?

Around 2000, the dot-com scandal revealed fundamental conflicts of interest between activities that used to be done by separate firms; taking companies public, trading and asset management respectively. So did the regulatory response to the dot-com scandal decree that investment banks must be prevented from having these conflicting activities under one roof? Not at all, they were merely forced to install Chinese walls – policed by their own risk and compliance staff.

In the crash of 2008, investment bankers at megabanks were found to be speculating with the savings that ordinary citizens had entrusted to the commercial division of that megabank. So have megabanks now been forced to break themselves up into two different parts – the high-risk investment division and the more traditional commercial division, which contains everyone's savings accounts and the payment system? Not at all, there is merely going to be an 'electrified ring fence' between the two arms – at least in the UK, and not now but in a few years' time.

Meanwhile the banks themselves have never offered full access to its staff to be interrogated about what went wrong and why, nor have banks said: we are kicking out everybody who in the recent past gambled with our capital buffers or our reputation. The banks have not broken with the accountancy firms

that missed or chose to miss all the erroneous or misleading
items on the banks' balance sheets and the same is true of the
credit rating agencies. Banks have certainly not joined hands to
fight for a globally enforced increase in capital buffers. Indeed,
they have spent millions in lobbying to keep that inevitable
increase in buffers as low as possible.

Virtually all big banks remain publicly listed or are doing
everything they can to get back on the stock exchange as soon
as possible. The system of zero job security continues to govern
the City and so do caveat emptor and the code of silence. The
three major credit rating agencies have kept their de facto cartel, as have the four accountancy firms – who continue to do
lucrative consultancy jobs for the banks they are meant to audit
independently.

Former Labour prime minister Tony Blair is making at
least £2.5 million a year as advisor to JP Morgan. Hector Sants,
who as chief regulator saw his sector suddenly collapse in 2008,
was offered a top job at the megabank Barclays. His estimated
'compensation' was £3 million a year.

Fucking hell.

I met a man in his late sixties who had recently retired
after a long career at one of the smaller credit rating agencies.
He seemed like a genuinely nice person and only after our interview did I see that he had thoughtfully sent me a text to say
that he'd be five minutes late.

I asked him what had it been like for him to see, on the eve
of his retirement, the financial system very nearly collapse and
take down the rest of us?

'I still get so angry when I think about it,' he said. Taking
a job at a rating agency had seemed a perfect match to him
when he was young: a good salary for a service of genuine value
for society. 'We need ratings to work out how safe a company
or an investment bond is, what the risk of default might be. If

you can't trust it, you shouldn't do business with it – it's that simple.'

Then it was September 15, 2008. 'It was terrifying,' he said with genuine emotion. 'Absolutely terrifying. We came so close to a global meltdown.' He was on holiday in the week Lehman went bust. 'I remember opening up the paper every day and going: "Oh my God." I was on my BlackBerry following events. Confusion, embarrassment, incredulity . . . I went through the whole gamut of human emotions. At some point my wife threatened to throw my BlackBerry in the lake if I didn't stop reading on my phone. I couldn't stop.'

The BlackBerry addict was not the only one to feel something close to complete panic during the crash. In fact, it is hard to overstate the fear and confusion that insiders felt when events were unfolding. This inarticulate terror went all the way up the chain of power. *The New York Times* described the 'urgent and unusual' meeting in Washington that took place during the crash, in which the Fed chairman laid out the 'potentially devastating ramifications' of the crisis to U.S. congressional leaders. As Democratic senator Charles E. Schumer recalled afterwards: 'You have the credit lines in America, which are the lifeblood of the economy, frozen. That hasn't happened before. It's a brave new world. You are in unchartered territory, but the one thing you do know is that you can't leave them frozen or the economy will just head south at a rapid rate.' As he spoke, he swooped his hand in a downwards motion. 'You know, we'd be lucky . . .' he said, and trailed off. 'Well, I'll leave it at that.' Or here is Nobel Prize–winning economist Paul Krugman, on what it must have been like for U.S. Treasury secretary Hank Paulson to look at the mayhem after he decided to let Lehman fail: 'This is the utter nightmare of an economic policymaker. You're sitting there, and you may have just made the decision that destroyed the world.

Absolutely terrifying moment.'

Several years on from the events of 2008, the BlackBerry addict was as afraid and angry as he was then. 'Each time I read about a new financial product, I think: "Uh-oh." Every new product is described in those same warm, fuzzy phrases: how great they are and how safe.' This is exactly how the banks first introduced CDOs and their toxic friends.

Sometimes he felt as if finance has reacted to the crisis the way a motorist might after a near-accident. 'There is the adrenaline surge directly after the lucky escape, followed by the huge shock when you realise what could have happened. But as the journey continues and the scene recedes in the rear view mirror, you tell yourself: maybe it wasn't that bad. The memory of your panic fades, and you even begin to misremember what happened. Was it really that bad?'

At this point in the interview he was really angry and when I pointed this out he became even angrier: 'If you had told people at the height of the crisis that years later we'd have had no fundamental changes, nobody would have believed you. Such was the panic and fear. But here we are. It's back to business as usual. We went from "We nearly died from this" to "We survived this."'

●

Anger is a complex emotion. It produces lots of energy and can be very useful if you know what it is you want to fight for. But anger plus powerlessness is a one-way street ending in depression.

Curiosity can be a reprieve, for a while at least. I decided to reread all the interviews and resolved to ask a new question: why aren't you doing anything? If a nuclear reactor in your neighbourhood was run according to the same short-termist principles as the big banks, wouldn't you hope employees at that nuclear plant would blow the whistle? Sure, most people in finance do not work in activities that can be fatal to the bank and the wider system. But many people can see what is problematic and almost everybody faces a number of fundamental conflicts of interest and perverse incentives – the relentless succession of scandals prove it.

Why do insiders fail to act? Or perhaps more constructively: how realistic is the hope that change will come from the inside? That was going to be the last big question for the blog and many readers in the comment section seemed to have made up their minds about the answer already: of course those greedy bastards are not going to change. Why would they?

The idea that people in the City are driven purely by greed is hopelessly popular, no doubt kept alive by all the media stories about bonuses as well as films like *Wall Street* and more recently *The Wolf of Wall Street*. But after quizzing interviewees on their motives, 'greed' seemed a highly inadequate explanation for their behaviour. In fact, I have come to believe that our focus on greed is the biggest mistake outsiders have made in the aftermath of Lehman's collapse.

At a party in London I got talking to a man who asked me if I was that Dutch guy doing research into the culture of banking. I said I was and showed him a few interviews on my phone – see, no names of banks or bankers. He worked in risk and compliance at one of the biggest megabanks in the world and began to complain about the never-ending torrent of contradictory or superfluous new rules for the banks, on a national, European and global level. He took a healthy swig of his beer – clearly not his first – and said: 'Every day I see things that are illegal. Nothing that can sink the bank but certainly stuff that you can go to jail for.'

Such as?

He hesitated for a moment. 'Ah well, fuck it. Annual results of "friendly" companies circulating on the trading floor before their official publication. Critical comments removed from reports about companies that we hope to list on the stock exchange . . .'

In other words, his job was to police the Chinese walls and that was, as he angrily put it, 'a joke.' After I got him another beer he repeated what many veterans had told me. Years ago the City had seemed such a great career. These days they kept where they worked to themselves. 'I know it sounds nostalgic,' he said. 'But it looked like good pay for a decent and useful job. In the beginning it was. A great atmosphere and enough flexibility when it came to kids, as long as you did your job well. Then the Americans took over my firm. We had to work insane hours. There were redundancy waves. In the old days there were parties every week for colleagues who had been with the firm 20 years, 30 years . . . That is over. All the veterans have been laid off and nobody of the new generation is staying with the same firm for a whole career.'

You might think: morose drunken talk. But the fundamental conflicts of interest he identified do exist and when I met him again a few times in a sober state his story remained the same.

Risk and compliance is disparaged not only by front-office bankers but by most insiders. In *Traders, Guns and Money*, former middle-office veteran Satyajit Das defines the department as those who 'keep lists of all documents that need to be shredded in case of a problem.'

This is almost the opposite of what the man at the party and others working in internal control functions signed up for. I want to do a good job, they claimed. But my own bank stops me from doing it.

Why, then, did they not sound the alarm? I looked up the

man I had met at the party one more time and his face almost contorted with frustration: 'What am I going to do, at 41? I have a mortgage, kids . . . Where is the demand for my skills outside the banks?'

So was he concerned he might be laid off? Now his expression turned grim. 'I have collected so much shit about them over the years. They know. If they fire me I am going to the regulator and they're all fucked.'

This bitter compliance officer is a typical representative of the group of financial workers you might call the 'teeth grinders.' Their answer to the question of why they continue with business as usual is not 'greed' but 'fear.' Then if you press them, they say: 'I'm stuck.'

The first time I heard a teeth grinder say this I thought it was rather pathetic. But having moved to London for the blog and lived among the English, I began to see what he meant. The key is the school system. What shocked me, as an outsider, is that a nation that sees itself as the inventor and guardian of the concept of 'fair play' also appears to accept that children of rich parents receive a better education than those whose parents are poor.

Only 7 per cent of British children go to a private school yet half to two thirds of the current medical, media, judicial, legal and civil service elite is privately educated. The most expensive of these schools charge tens of thousands of pounds a year, per child, after taxes. A staggering number of British top politicians come from those schools, from both left and right. And then I started to notice that lots of prominent commentators – even those on the left – also went to top private schools such as Eton and, of course, end up sending their children too.

Perhaps this is why the issue is so relatively low on the public agenda? How do you agitate against a practice that you are taking part in yourself?

That's the trap for aspirational British parents. Some of the state schools are good enough not to spoil your chances of going to a top university. But in order to qualify for those you must live in the catchment area and – as British readers will already know – those houses are astronomically expensive.

To make matters even worse, London has managed to blow an even bigger housing bubble than Amsterdam. Some banking staff receive discounts on their mortgage but that benefit disappears if they are dismissed. Many banking staff do not have skills that are in high demand elsewhere in the economy and even if they find a new job their pay is likely to be at least 20 per cent lower. Can you still afford the school fees after taking such a cut?

That is how stuck parents are with children of school-going age, particularly in London. Risk and compliance staff have nowhere near the income for a place at Eton or some other top school. But a minimum of £5,000 a year per child at a less prestigious place is a heavy financial burden all the same – especially since the costs do not stop at the school fees but include uniforms, school trips and so on.

The man who admitted at the party to looking the other way as colleagues committed financial crimes had walked into this trap. It could be a coincidence but of those interviewees in control functions who later emailed to say they had left the sector of their own accord, none of them had children.

•

There are people in the City who long for a better system. That is the gist of the message sent by the teeth grinders and something similar came out of a second type of financial worker. They too were struggling with the ethical dilemmas in their workplace but had chosen not to act on them, not so much out of fear or because they were stuck, but for other reasons. You could define this group as the 'neutrals' and I would run into them across the City, outside the banks and in them, and in the back, middle and front office.

The human resources officer who came forward to discuss a 'part of banking that's not really seen' is a fine example. 'It can be quite arbitrary, the redundancies,' she said at one point. 'I go over the list with managers. Women on maternity leave are often the first to go. People who are absent due to illness.' Next a sip of wine, followed by: 'God, my job sounds awful when put like this. But I do love it, the adrenaline, the challenges, a good tussle with an exceptionally good employment lawyer. Intellectual chess. Some of the most exceptional people in the world work in finance.'

She was making around £100,000 a year, which she characterised as 'an obscene amount, absolutely. You can have three or four nurses working for that.' The flipside, she continued, was that 'I deal with people who make even more. I look at them, I see what they do, I look at my own skill set, and frankly, it's often better. I live quite frugally, save a lot. I'd like to continue to live in London; I have really taken to this city. That means I have to make a lot of money.'

The senior regulator is a typical neutral, too, and so is the rock-'n'-roll trader. Let's say experienced traders like me can make anywhere between £300,000 and £1 million a year, he said. 'Meanwhile, somebody fighting for our country in Afghanistan is making £22,000. It's funny how that works. When you ask me if that's fair, I also think of the guy who is making £5 million, while I know I am smarter than he is. Life isn't fair.'

'I do wonder sometimes,' said a dealmaker in corporate finance who could expect to make well over £1 million a year. 'What is the difference between a surgeon and me? The surgeon probably works as hard as I do, and he or she actually saves lives. So why do I get paid so much more? The answer is that the surgeon can only operate on a set number of patients each day. Their work is not scalable. The bank is paid a percentage of the deals we do. The workload for a deal worth £200 million may be pretty similar to one worth £1 billion. But the fee is much higher, though not five times.'

This was how neutrals justified their compensation. They went over all the ethical dilemmas only to conclude: what am I, as a lone individual, to do? Yes, my bank and hence my job would have ceased to exist without taxpayer support. Now I am receiving a fat bonus. That is absurd. Now, what would you do in my place?

The million-dollar banker whose job so resembled that of a journalist – 'only better' – considered himself 'centre left' politically. I told him that I understood his job to be a useful activity that required hard work while meeting a real need in the economy. But did he himself think that he deserved the million-dollar bonus he had earned the year before?

He shrugged. 'Do I think the balance between skill and pay is right? If a client is managing a £10 billion fund and you stop him from making a mistake that would have cost him 2 per cent, and you do that two or three times a year . . . that is worth a lot.'

He looked into the distance, finished his beer and asked: 'Do you and I deserve to live in the first world?'

What distinguished neutrals from teeth grinders was not any real difference of opinion about all that is going wrong in finance. What set them apart was that they had made their peace with the system in its current form and the rewards they were receiving. They would say something like: 'I am giving my job the full 100 per cent and I am enjoying it because it is immensely challenging and interesting in intellectual terms. I have nothing to be ashamed of personally and so I refuse to apologise for it.' I really believe that neutrals were speaking the truth when they claimed not to break any rules themselves or abuse their power at the expense of ignorant clients. In any case, neutrals were the kind of sources every researcher dreams of: free of the resentment and anger that seemed to gnaw at many teeth grinders and whistle blowers. Nor were they caught in a cycle of self-congratulatory defensiveness: why does nobody admit how great we are?

And as I spoke to more and more neutrals I began to understand why it was so easy for them to go with the flow. How would it help if they took a stand, they'd ask. 'I'd lose my job never to find a new one anywhere in the City. Meanwhile nothing would have changed.'

Compare it to your CO_2 emissions, a few of the neutrals said. 'You can turn your life upside-down to make

it climate neutral. Has that solved the problem? Not in the least. But your own life is now a complete mess.'

I accept that as an individual I am powerless, neutrals would say, and I do what I can not to make things worse. 'Greed' seemed entirely inadequate as an explanation for this line of thinking and, indeed, many neutrals suggested they could make far more money but had chosen not to.

The rock-'n'-roll trader was earning at least half a million a year, yet he said that sometimes his job could feel like 'a very expensive prison term.' Even though a job outside the City would pay only a fraction of his current income he did not expect to work there for much longer. Nor would he wish to see his children go into finance. 'I wouldn't feel they're adding anything. I find myself more and more interested in people who have built something. My life has revolved around a number on a screen for more than 10 years now. It can't be healthy to trade a number on a screen for your entire life, can it?'

It's much easier to talk about career-changing steps than to take them, obviously. On the other hand, when I met again with the sales trader who had dismissed the bonus ritual as 'theatrics,' I could see with my own eyes that, at least for some, the cliché of 'money-grabbing greedy bankers' simply won't do.

In his first interview the sales trader had told me how after travelling widely as a student in a particular region of the world he had 'rolled into' the sector. For well over a decade now he was advising a small group of big investors, such as pension funds. This meant passing on research about 'his' region, carried out by analysts similar to the million-dollar banker, as well as being available for advice. 'Say a virus breaks out at a major cattle corporation; will this pass or [could it] take down the company? My clients speak to 10 or 15 banks each day, then form their own view.'

During the boom years before 2008, he'd often find handouts from estate agents in his mailbox: 'City bonus, don't know what to do with it?' Something happens to your brain after a big bonus, he had found. 'You think, wow, so this is what I am worth. That term in itself is telling: "worth."'

The first time we had met was in a restaurant but this time he had invited me over to his place for dinner, giving me the chance to see for myself that he had never 'upgraded' his life by moving into an expensive house. Nor did he have children. Over a cup of tea he talked about the very best part of his job: arranging trips to companies in his region. 'To travel halfway around the world with clients whom I have come to know really well over the years. To see countries and companies change . . . Can you see why I love my job?'

That is your chief asset for an equity sales trader like him, he said: the relationship with your clients. 'When you move employers, you take them with you, so when a bank poaches you, they poach your clients.'

We had some more tea and I asked how many times he had done that – hopping between jobs by letting a bank poach him?

Laughing, he explained that actually, he had never done such a thing, not even once, and this had made him a real exception at his bank. 'Looking back on the day I started, not a single person from that trading floor is still with the bank. Those 300 research analysts, traders and sales people . . . all have moved on, either made redundant or left on their own accord.'

Changing employers would be 'a sideways step' for him, not a step up, he said. He'd make more because that's how it works; you are lured away by a better offer. But what would he gain? 'I'd spend 18 months proving myself, working twice as hard, getting to know colleagues and building relationships with them.'

Not that his loyalty worked in his favour at the bank, he emphasised. 'It makes bankers look almost weird when they don't hop from bank to bank. It's like top people look at their CVs and go: what's wrong with this guy? When it comes to promotions, there is this bias in favour of getting an outsider. The idea is, this guy must have been passed over for promotions a few times, so giving him one now looks like we couldn't find anyone better.'

Over a final cup of tea he said that working in the City is a real buzz. At the same time, he went on, 'it can seriously challenge one's sense of level-headedness. I have tremendously enjoyed it so far because of the relationships I have built and the things I have learned. It can be over from one day to the next. You receive a risk premium for that. Today is my time; tomorrow, somebody else's.'

•

Interviews with neutrals were among the most pleasant and rewarding and many of the errors in the architecture of the financial sector became apparent through their stories. They did nothing to change things but had a very sharp eye when it came to identifying all that was going wrong.

What a contrast to the 'Master of the Universe' bankers. They had a rather different answer to the question of why they did not sound the alarm.

10

Masters of the Universe

'Big deals are quite a journey and you develop a kind of broth-er-in-arms friendship with clients and with colleagues at other banks working on the same deal . . . You start out with the client and your team looking pristine, presenting your slick-looking pitch. Then come the negotiations, stress, travel, late-night meetings, you decide to start smoking again . . . Months later you have been in a room together for 24 hours. Your shirt is un-buttoned, you stink, you plunge into the inevitable last-minute negotiations with the lawyers, it goes on and on, and then . . . You sign. It's real and dirty, a very masculine thing, if you will. The war stories: "You remember when the client said this, and you said that . . . ?"'

This is a former managing director talking me through the listing of a new company on the stock exchange. Until he fell into a depression and dropped out, he had been a classic 'Master of the Universe' banker. To my surprise, this type of banker seemed perfectly happy with the name, even though Tom Wolfe coined it in *Bonfire of the Vanities* in the eighties to satirise the overwheening confidence of the ambitious young men who racked up millions on Wall Street. Many Master of the Universe bankers did not seem to know the providence of their nickname, nor did they seem to care. Neither for the literature nor for the irony.

That said, whenever they described their work I couldn't help but feel a sense of recognition, affinity even. Initially, at least. 'Doing a deal is like scoring a goal,' said the former managing director dealmaker, 'or maybe for journalists, getting a scoop.' People spoke in all seriousness of experiencing something akin to an 'orgasm' or 'something narcotic' after landing a deal. 'Walking into the bank on the day that you know a congratulatory email has gone out saying: "Listen everyone, so and so had done really well" is fabulous. People stop you in the corridor and emails flood in. You feel on top of the world.'

This, I have to admit, is a pretty accurate description of me the day after I 'made' the front page of the *Guardian* for the first time. The sense of pride and even elation was intense; colleagues who had previously ignored me suddenly remembered who I was.

If neutrals spoke of their work as a daily puzzle and 'ultimately just a job,' Master of the Universe bankers spoke as though more was at stake. Their office persona was strongly aligned with their ego and sense of self-worth and they thought of their work as a race or a match where they could prove themselves.

Deeply competitive, they clearly enjoyed what they did and seemed to relish a good battle. 'Work hard, play hard' was their motto and they frequently used combative terms in their speech: 'If you want to get ahead in this place you need to be *aggressive* and prepared to always *push* yourself further.'

'The sorts of deals we do are very, very important to our clients,' said a veteran dealmaker. 'Crudely put, we can make them very rich. Often they construct contracts in such a way that the better the price they get, the more we are rewarded.

Clients across three time zones expect me to be on call 24/7 throughout the year. I may get a call and have to go straight to the airport to fly who knows where. In negotiations you wear each other out first, and only at the very last moment you make concessions. So most negotiations go on for a long time and are concluded in the evening, at night or on weekends. I can be coming home from work just as the alarm goes off and my wife and kids are getting up.'

People spoke of their job as 'the most challenging and excitingontheplanet'andaboutadeepsenseofcamaraderie   with like-minded colleagues. The word 'friendship' rarely appeared, let alone 'solidarity.' Asked for similes many mentioned sports and war. A team working for months on a deal is a 'special forces unit' while the trading floor with all its screens is like the trenches: 'Bullets flying over your head, with the traders in the role of gunners and juniors as medics and supply guys.'

My first Master of the Universe interviewee had had a first-class career in finance. In her late thirties, she was of Asian descent and having grown up in the British middle class she had gone to a top university to be recruited straight away by a top bank.

People like me have been trained to process information in seconds, she said. 'We are the Olympic athletes of information and it's a race to see who can get there first. It's also a fight.' She had started out as a research analyst in a big bank where she had five minutes to come out with her view after any significant news. This was transmitted to the whole global investment community by the sales team as fast as possible. 'My physical and mental state changes when I see an important piece of news, she said, adding: 'Sometimes my body feels it before I can even think.'

You need to realise the power and influence an analyst at one of the most prestigious banks in the world has, she said as her voice grew more and more animated: 'If I changed my recommendation from "neutral" to "buy" for a particular company I was following, the stock could rise by 5 per cent. I'd know that I had just made its investors and maybe that company's CEO millions.'

She looked me in the eye and asked: 'Say you hear at this moment that Israel is about to attack Iran. What do you do?' I thought for a moment before saying: 'I don't know, call home to check on my loved ones?' She gave a surprised laugh, almost as if I'd caught her out. 'Well, you see, you live in the real world. The first thing I think is: buy call options on oil as there may be disruptions in supply, buy U.S. defence stocks and other companies that have military contracts. Next my brain goes into unbelievable tangents. How does this change prior assumptions and valuations on my investments? Every single outcome of an Israeli attack goes through my head, all of which I assign probabilities. Who will do the rebuilding? If the regime becomes pro-American that'll probably be Halliburton, so that's a buy opportunity. And so on.'

After her time with the bank she had moved to a hedge fund where she invested and managed other people's money. This is where the smartest people in finance work, she confided. 'They feel superior to investment bankers. First, the top people in hedge funds makes far more than CEOs at banks. Second, hedge funds use investment banks to trade – making bankers dependent on them for business and commissions. Third, "hedgies" feel superior to bankers because the former put their money where their mouth is. Banks are too big to fail, she said, whereas in hedge funds you lose money and you're out.'

Finance is such an extremely challenging and stimulating environment, she said happily. 'So many smart people, such efficiency all around. I have stayed in five-star hotels since I was 21. Flown business class. Dated someone with a private jet . . .'

This was the Master of the Universe in full flow and here my identification with them came to an end – and not only because none of my girlfriends had owned a private jet.

The key difference is the reward and incentive structure. Journalists may worry about their articles reaching a certain level of online traffic but it's not the be all and end all; in investment banking, by contrast, your work can always be boiled down to a number. How many deals for IPOs, mergers and acquisitions did your team win and how much did the bank make off them? How many trades did you do? What was the profit generated by the complex products you built or sold? How much money did investors entrust to you as asset manager?

If you can measure 'performance' you can start comparing yourself to colleagues and this is what happens in the City – constantly. Remember the job titles that once sounded like code? Across the City there must be around 10 to 15 'mergers and acquisitions telecom Middle East North Africa' bankers with the rank of director, and the same is true of 'equity derivatives structurers' at the level of vice-president for the European market. Nearly everyone fits into one such niche and specialised companies keep league tables and rankings of each one: how each bank is 'performing,' how each team in that bank and each individual in that team is doing. This pervasive ranking allows Master of the Universe bankers to experience their job not just as if they are competing in a daily race or match but also as if they are in a long-running premiership or permanent tournament.

The world of finance is a meritocracy, people high up in their ranking would tell me. 'Ronaldo, Messi and other top footballers make enormous amounts of money, too, don't they? Well, I am the Messi of mergers and acquisitions pharmaceuticals Europe.'

Neutrals would struggle to say this without cracking up

but Masters of the Universe would make this claim without even a hint of irony. Books by and for insiders such as *Monkey Business: Swinging through the Wall Street Jungle* and *Damn, It Feels Good to Be a Banker* make the same point: the world of finance is a meritocracy.

Look around you, Masters of the Universe would declare proudly. 'The City is home to literally every nationality, every group of social class you can imagine. Around here everybody gets a shot but only the very best survive. I am one of those and that is the best feeling in the world.'

When I confronted the Master of the Universe with all the criticism of the sector, the same arguments surfaced that the neutrals used: the work I am doing is useful, legal and of vital importance to the economy of London and Great Britain. There was a difference, though. Masters of the Universe ran down this list of justifications almost absent-mindedly, like an athlete absorbed in her training schedule for the next Olympics having to explain to yet another journalist why human rights violations in the host country should not lead to a boycott.

Often, Masters of the Universe would be irritated or even offended. What is so difficult to understand, they would ask: are you just jealous, or one of those who prefer to lead their lives in mediocrity?

After everything I had learnt, their pride in their jobs sounded to me like a clear case of denial and self-delusion. But as soon as I made a subtle suggestion to that effect the interview changed markedly. Contrary to teeth grinders and neutrals, Masters of the Universe took criticism of the sector personally and quickly our conversation would become more like verbal wrestling or intellectual chess. I would 'open' with a piece of criticism and they would respond with their countermove.

The super quant who earlier described the scope for mis-understandings with non-quants was a prototype Master of the Universe. In his mid fifties, funny, straight-talking, totally unpretentious, he reminded of stall vendors at Amsterdam's biggest open fruit, vegetable and textile market. He stocked up on cola light and coffee and began to take the piss out of me for ordering cranberry juice.

'I have the wrong accent,' he explained. 'I went to a shit school . . . Forty years ago I wouldn't even have been given an interview in the City. Finance today is fiercely meritocratic. Doesn't matter if you're gay or black or working-class, if you can do something better than the other person, you'll move up.'

My career is basically the meritocratic system in its full glory, he said. This was why he found the cliché of investment banks as casinos or gambling houses immensely irritating and he had volunteered for interview in order to 'offer a more measured assessment.' He snorted at the idea that they are a bunch of gamblers. 'There's no point for the bank to have somebody punting around and making us £50 million in one year only to lose the same amount the next. We call those the "lucky monkeys" and my bank is working very, very hard not to hire those and to get rid of the ones who had slipped through the net.'

He continued: 'There's probably more introspection in finance than anywhere else. You know who are most terrified of lucky monkeys? The traders and risk takers themselves. They are terrified of being just a lucky monkey and constantly ask themselves: was it luck? What's going on? Have we missed something?'

More cola and then: 'The vast majority of those working in financial services are decent, honourable people doing decent and honourable things.'

This was almost like an invitation for a debate. At the time we spoke we were in the middle of yet another banking scandal where many traders at many banks had not behaved decently or honourably at all. 'Rotten apples,' he said with a shrug. Wouldn't happen at his bank.

How about the excessively risky products in the years before 2008? Another dismissive gesture. 'Remember there's a lot of peer-pressure in a bank. If you've got somebody swinging around taking big risks, everybody will say: "That's not right. If this guy loses us £100 million, I won't have a bonus."' Bankers at a division that has run up big losses for the bank become 'pariahs,' he said.

I brought up the huge bonuses and exorbitant pay. In a free market, competition on price should drive down wages because the bank paying out the least in 'compensation' can charge the lowest prices. That is how the free market works, right? He conceded that in finance today there are high 'barriers to entry'; it has become very difficult to start a new bank, if only because due to all the rules you need an immense army of risk and compliance officers. 'Frankly,' he said about all the new rules that have come in since 2008, they are 'very expensive to comply with and 90 per cent of them are utterly useless.'

Anyway, he went on: 'The libertarian in me says: if it were possible to do banking for less, somebody would do it. This is just how much it costs.'

And so he swept every piece of criticism of the sector off the table: it wasn't the fault of the sector or of the banks, or of his own bank, or of people like him in his bank. The crash? A perfect storm due to market-distorting government policies and the incompetence of the mega insurance company AIG.

What's more, he said: some events have an extremely low probability but an extreme impact if they do happen. 'At 8:45 a.m. on September 11, 2001, the chance of two aeroplanes hitting the World Trade Centre would be indistinguishable from zero. Then it happened.'

•

Are Master of the Universe types really this self-assured? I was given the opportunity to look behind the façade just once. It started with an email:

'Do you speak to happy bankers at all? Your interviewees all seem so . . . miserable.'

We met for lunch in a restaurant on Canary Wharf surrounded by hundreds of people dividing their attention between the food on their plate, the person sitting opposite them, and their phone (or phones). He was a salesman aged around 45 with the rank of director and worked for a megabank in 'treasury sales.' To manage its internal cash flows his bank had developed special instruments which the happy banker sold as products to companies and other financial institutions.

We ordered our food and he said that my blog was making him 'a little worried. Readers get a distorted picture of finance. There are many happy bankers out there. I love my job and I think treasury is useful, too. We manage and hedge the bank's risks, and help clients manage theirs; who could be against that?'

He shrugged his shoulders: 'Some on your blog are so negative about the sector . . . It's not very kind to say, but they just didn't make it. They get kicked out and then they go complain to the media. It's tough to take, obviously. You had to go while your colleague is still at his desk. Because he was better. Getting sacked at a bank is like getting dumped by a woman who says: "It's not me, it's you."'

The 'competitive element' had attracted him to banking and he found the meritocratic culture irresistible, 'knowing that those who don't make the grade get cut. I'm the kind of person who wants to swim with sharks and see if I can survive. To feel myself grow when challenged by harsh, achievement-driven standards. Happy bankers are those who don't do it for the money but for the thrill.'

At university he was a dropout but his bank had never even asked him about his qualifications. Nor had he ever encountered racism, sexism or homophobia. 'The simple reason is that people just don't give a fuck who you are. It's what you can do.'

He stopped talking for a moment and, as I caught up on my note-taking, I remember thinking: fascinating, a genuine 25-carat Master of the Universe. Almost everyone in his bank were fine and decent people, he insisted. 'Yes, you have the odd evil exception. Why don't banks kick these out? Well, as long as they make money for the banks that's really hard to do.'

With a grin he began to talk about a dinner he had gone to the other day. 'People from different walks of life. A woman asked me what I did for a living. Now, I know that some colleagues try to hide they are bankers, but that's not my style. So we were sitting in a group and before me this guy said: "I am a surgeon." That went down very well with some of the ladies, obviously. When my turn came I said I was a banker. A fierce discussion broke out with people saying, look at that surgeon, now he is doing something useful. And I went: "I think banking is just as useful." So this woman next to me explodes into a tirade about bankers being parasites and what have you. She really had a go at me, but under the table her hand was riding up the inside of my thigh. It's an irresistible mix for some women; this idea of bankers as rich and evil bad boys.'

That was the happy banker. I sent over a draft version of his words, he removed an anecdote about a failed deal that might be traced back to him but just before I was going to publish his interview he sent me an email. Could I wait?

We agreed to meet again, this time in the aptly named Le

Coq d'Argent. It is an expensive roof-terrace bar and restaurant overlooking the former stock exchange in the heart of the old City. A few weeks earlier a banker had committed suicide by jumping from the roof and a high fence had just been installed.

Suicide was not on the happy banker's mind but it was a different person sitting before me. The week before we met he had received 'the call.' Only when he was standing outside the office phoning his wife to say he had been made redundant had he allowed himself to feel something. 'Telling her what happened and what this meant for us financially. Only then did I become emotional, when I felt the impact this would have on my family. I went back into the office a few days later, to help a few people out with outstanding stuff, and I could tell they had had a pep talk about having been spared. I remember those, after earlier waves.'

We ordered another coffee – he was no longer a busy man. 'Perhaps I already sensed what was coming,' he suggested, referring to our earlier interview. 'Maybe the decision had been made already by top management and I had unconsciously picked up on it? Maybe I was mentally preparing myself when talking to you the way I did.'

He said that looking back now he may have fallen victim to the 'self-serving idea that we control our fate; as long as you're good, nothing bad can happen to you, and since nothing bad has happened to me, it must mean I am good and therefore safe; that sort of thing. In the same way military men tell themselves that they can't die because they don't make mistakes. But the best soldier can drive over a land mine.'

It had gone exactly as he had thought it would. 'My boss called me on my desk and something was up with his voice; could I come down to the first floor? It felt like I was walking up to the firing squad.'

They had given him the bad news right away, just like he

knew they would, even using the time-tested formula of 'it's not you, it's us.' There were several people of his rank for a shrinking number of positions, they told him. The others had more experience.

They were immensely practical, he said, outlining the procedure in clear steps. And then that was it. He said he was proud of how he had held himself together. 'Taking it on the chin, not getting emotional, maintaining a professional approach. In fact my boss said: "When my time comes I hope I'll have the presence of mind to take the news like you have."'

He understood why the bank had blocked his phone and email the moment the meeting with his boss began. 'I might go nuts and call clients, send off a string of crazy emails to them, or to the CEO . . . All the client contracts are in the office, their files . . . I can see why someone is immediately cordoned off when made redundant; his presence can only be disruptive.'

As he was packing his personal belongings under the watchful eye of a security guard, a colleague who hadn't heard yet came up to him for some business-related issue. 'So, I actually had to tell him: "Look, I've just been made redundant." Then he asked me for help on something; effectively a handover chat.' The happy banker let out a sigh and said in a forgiving voice, 'Clumsiness, of course.' A few minutes later he was standing outside with his stuff and a blocked security pass, calling his wife.

He said he was no longer in touch with colleagues, socially. 'Going out we'd mainly talk about work; what would be the point? Also, there's this mercenary quality to life in an investment bank. Given how tough things have got in the industry people are careful about bonding; it can be over in a minute.'

We could hear by the noise of the cars beneath that rush hour was approaching and around us on the roof terrace the first few smartly dressed people were filing in for cocktail hour.

When I ordered another round of coffees they came with more of those delicious cookies to justify the crazy price.

'Obviously I am really sorry for what happened,' I started out, slightly gingerly. 'But you will agree that this is a really interesting laboratory experiment.' I hesitated again but if you want to 'swim with the sharks' you should be able to handle a painful question. 'Earlier, you said that only the best survive in investment banks. Now you have been let go . . .'

The look in his eyes nearly made me regret having said anything. 'I still do not think investment banking is a terrible environment. It's not for everyone, sure, but it's my natural state. Research shows that the life of a wild animal is mostly suffering: stress and fear and pain. Yet do we believe pets to be happier? I'd rather be the wild animal.'

•

Sometimes when I saw Masters of the Universe throw their money around in London I would think of the happy banker and his sudden discovery of his own vulnerability. We kept in touch though I never found out if he had changed his mind about the health of the sector.

In fact it was interesting how ready the Masters of the Universe were to publicly defend their industry, even those who had been personally burnt by it. I have mentioned before that discussions with Masters of the Universe felt like debating contests – a good example of this was when we let the super quant free on the comment thread under my blog. The *Guardian* editor had chosen 'The vast majority of those working in financial services are decent people' as a headline and the quote did not go down well with many readers. Over 500 comments came in, many of them angry and highly critical, and it took less than an hour for somebody to bring up the Holocaust.

The comment thread stayed open for 72 hours and the super quant threw himself in to the debate, without ever resorting to personal attacks or fallacies – which marked him out from his less disciplined opponents.

Afterwards I emailed him to ask if he had enjoyed it. It was actually really addictive, he responded; only when he realised it was 2 a.m. and that he had an important meeting a few hours later had he managed to pull himself away.

He did wonder though about the use of 'debates' like this, though: 'I expected the visceral hard speak – the internet makes that a very low-risk/cost thing to spout insults and hate when you aren't in physical proximity – but the lack of understanding of the function and process of banking was more surprising,' he wrote. 'To use an analogy: there are arguments as to why boxing should be a banned sport but I felt like people were saying, "Boxing should be banned because it takes place underwater and so people drown all the time." So the argument degenerates into arguing that boxing isn't an underwater sport rather than focusing on the real issues. I felt the real anthropological insight was into people's reactions rather than the banking industry itself.'

This was the Master of the Universe at his best: prepared to give all and immensely keen to win each and every discussion, but without cheating. Hence the super quant's adamant opposition to banks that are 'too big to fail.' This was the one issue he felt required immediate reform: what is the point of a game if you cannot lose?

If change in finance is going to come from within it will not be from Masters of the Universe. It takes little imagination to see an alpha, highly competitive Master of the Universe type trying to sell as many hyper-complex financial products as she can, or casting a sideways glance on the league table and mumbling 'caveat emptor' while she 'rips the face off' a small pension fund or municipality 'somewhere in Europe,'

How could Masters of the Universe blow the whistle on the many conflicts of interest and perverse incentives across the sector if they refuse to acknowledge them in the first place?

Still, you could see this type of banker would be just as happy and fulfilled in a sector which is organised differently. After all, they are driven not by a deep need for money but for status. They are like athletes ready to sacrifice everything for a gold medal – not out of an obsession with that precious metal but because winning means standing on the podium, hearing the anthem and thinking: I am the best.

You have Masters of the Universe in journalism too; they involve their egos in everything they do, can be a pain to work with and take criticism of the media extremely personally. Their work is often among the most valuable in the newsroom.

One thing you can say for the Masters of the Universe is that at least they still feel the need to engage in dialogue and justify themselves. Others seemed to have no desire to connect with the outside world at all.

11

Life in the Bubble

For typical 'blinkered bankers,' work is not the ordeal it is for teeth grinders. It is not 'just a job' like for neutrals nor the glorious championship Masters of the Universe make out of it. For blinkered bankers their work has quite simply become their world.

This type could be approached only informally: striking up a chance conversation in a bar or on a plane or being seated next to one at a 'dinner party,' as the English call them. These were difficult and frustratingly short exchanges for no sooner did I bring up the crash and all the scandals – let alone the financial sector's moral responsibility to society – then the conversation would break down. 'Nobody forced people to take out loans that they must have known were far beyond their means.' Or: 'Politicians are to blame, they distorted the market by subsidising home ownership.' And: 'I can't remember hearing complaints when house prices were going up. Did you?'

At that point I would say truthfully and as diplomatically as my blunt Dutch nature allowed that yes, blaming 'the bankers' for everything seems an important and under-discussed part of the problem. Having said that, it is also possible to see deep-seated issues across the sector . . .

Teeth grinders and neutrals would respond with an observation, elaboration or correction while Masters of the Universe pointed out patiently that I had fallen for the banker-bashers' propaganda. Blinkered bankers did not respond at all. It was as if even a mildly critical suggestion was enough to place me outside their circle, much like fanatical fans of a football club who hear you are from their rival's hometown. Still, it was possible to study this type of banker, through those who worked or lived with them and also with the help of people who admitted: I used to be like that until I fell into depression, was made redundant or left abandoned by my partner and I was finally forced back into 'the real world.'

The process happens in a deceptively gradual way, interviewees said, and it starts with the hours. For a number of years you are permanently sleep-deprived while spending pretty much every waking hour in the office. Many are told literally: 'You cannot afford to be ill in this job.' So no matter how you feel you drag yourself into the office. You are five minutes late after working until 2 a.m. the night before? For juniors, that means being screamed at.

Face time is the term: making sure your boss sees the hours you are putting in. Particularly in dealmaking, which regularly demands 'pulling an all-nighter': you work till 7 a.m., take a taxi home to shower and change and then the same taxi back to the office. 'I thought I'd never cope with the lack of sleep,' said an intern who had just spent a few months in a dealmaking team at a top bank. 'It's amazing how you adapt. I have my dips, around 4 p.m. usually, but I manage. I come in by 9 a.m. and go out around midnight, but 3 a.m. is no exception either. When I have been able to get home before midnight for a few days in a row, I think to myself: Wow, lucky me. Same if I haven't had to work for three weekends in a row.'

Your superior can claim you at any time, weekends included, so you can never plan or work towards a moment when you know you'll be able to relax. You become familiar with that knot in your stomach when you are with friends or your loved one and the red light on the BlackBerry starts flashing. 'From that moment on, you have to check it, you have to know if something important has come up,' said a former dealmaking banker who had decided after two years it wasn't for her. When she'd go out to dinner with her investment banker friends on a weeknight there would be an agreed moment when all of them checked their phones. You are treated as indispensable and you have to drop everything as and when the bank needs you. But the next moment you can be fired and marched out of the building within five minutes. So all of a sudden the bank *can* cope with your unavailability?

What happens in such an environment is that people try to outdo each other, juniors said. There are cockfights over who has sacrificed most. A junior tells his managing director he even missed his grandmother's funeral to work on a deal. The MD immediately fires back: 'I missed my father-in-law's funeral!'

You are on a business trip when you hear an important member of your family has suffered a serious accident. Your boss offers to fly you back but he does so in such a way that you understand how much kudos you'll get by staying. So you stay and hope your family member will be OK. Or you miss the wedding of one of your best friends. Or even the birth of your child. Your parents fly in all the way from Australia, Argentina or Singapore and your boss makes you work so much you hardly see them.

The dealmaker who had left her job of her own accord said without apparent resentment that her two years had been extremely valuable to her: 'How to handle stress and all the monkey tasks they make you do. But the real lessons were personal: how quickly you can forget yourself, and how easily you become the worst version of yourself.'

She grew up in Asia where she had been exposed to extreme poverty from a very early age. You would expect someone with my background to remain grounded, she reflected. But her job had made her feel so frustrated that she was liable to explode at the slightest issue. 'I was permanently stressed, and this carried over to the rest of my life: the chocolate getting stuck in the vending machine, the taxi showing up late, being stranded in traffic – it took very little to provoke a reaction.'

The life of a young investment banker is such that you become entirely self-absorbed and self-centred, she had found. 'You forget there's a world out there with real problems.'

It is a combination of an endurance game and a war of attrition, interviewees said. The hazing goes on for years and by the end of it you will have lost your friends outside the sector, because there comes a point when you cancel at the very last moment again and they give up on you. Relationships? A sex life is quite possible, yes – but a love life?

A young sales trader at a megabank talked about love over lunch in a fast food sushi restaurant near St Paul's Cathedral. A maths graduate in his mid twenties, he described his family background as 'British working class.' At his university all the big corporations had come to deliver their 'pitches.' He saw the starting salary at banks, realised he was £20,000 in student debt and went for it. 'It seemed a no-brainer,' he said, having no real idea at the time what a job on a trading floor might be like. 'I just saw the figure.' That was a few years ago. Now he would catch himself looking at his colleague next to him, a father in his early thirties who gets in around 6:30 a.m. and doesn't leave the office until seven or eight in the evening. All to offer his children a better future, his colleague had told him. 'I hear him on the phone to his children three times a day.

That is his contact with them.'

He said that since taking this job, the 'people who love me say they have seen me change.' And his girlfriend? That relationship is still young, he said, so she did not know him before he became a banker. She was not with a bank but she, too, had to work till 'stupid o'clock.' Most employers pay for a cab home if you work after 9 p.m. This was often the only time they talked, on the phone, each in their own taxi. Could this hold? 'No way will your girlfriend stick around if you're never there,' he noted. 'Unless she likes the trade-off; you have no time for me but you buy me expensive stuff. What kind of relationship is that? And if you lose your job she dumps you.'

Soon after the interview this sales trader quit his job. Others keep going on the assumption that this is not forever. And they are right. Around your early thirties the extreme hours are over, giving you the chance to resume your friendships and contacts outside the sector. Except at this point the financial gap with the rest of society is becoming unbridgeable.

You have to imagine, said the junior: you are 22 years old and you are making £45,000 plus bonus. A year after graduating.

The trouble is, within six months you are used to it. 'I would spend £250 on a night out and think nothing of it,' said another dealmaker who quit his job after two years. 'I would spend £100 on dinner and genuinely think to myself: well, that was not too expensive.'

The CDO banker said that he was making more in one year than his father did in a quarter of a century. How did he respond? I asked. 'I couldn't tell him, could I? My background is blue-collar, my father worked on the shipping yards. Had I told my friends, they'd think I had committed fraud.'

Your income sets you apart from everyone else, people said, and so does the luxurious lifestyle. The head of marketing who chose a City career because she needed a double income as a single mother said: 'You get ridiculously fastidious, what airline to fly, where to eat.'

A junior dealmaker who had left his bank on his own initiative remembered how colleagues were always on the phone making reservations: 'Table for four here, table for six there. The restaurant business in London must love bankers. Some guys would come in on Mondays with the bills from the weekend. Dropping £1,000 on a night out was not surprising.'

Kilian Wawoe was a senior human resources officer in the asset management division of ABN Amro in the Netherlands and Monaco before writing a very critical book about the bonus culture and moving into academia. He had flown business class a lot and this had a peculiar effect on him. 'Over there, a line of sweaty people and you walk past all that, with your platinum card. Have you noticed that people in business class are far more likely to look at passengers making their way to economy? They want to be seen to be sitting in business class. I never catch people in the first rows of economy doing that.'

For many years Wawoe was the person to give bankers their bonus. 'I have seen people change after a bonus, seen them become unhappy. Suddenly their benchmark changed, they began to compare themselves to a whole different set of people. When I started out at the bank I did not get a bonus, nor expected one. In later years I got €1000, which I really enjoyed. A little extra. A few years later I went to work for the bank in Monaco, where they promised me a €5,000 bonus if I did well. At the end of my assignment I got €30,000 and you know what? I felt cheated.'

The employee relations manager who spoke so eloquently about the ins and outs of firing bankers had previously worked in other industries. People get much, much less there when they are made redundant, she said. 'Still I get people at the bank telling me, literally: "I am offended by your offer of £300,000." I hear people say, about someone on a £125,000 salary plus £300,000 bonus a year: "I don't know how people survive on that." They mean it.'

Most people in finance are moulded by the system, she had found. 'They morph. I morph. The other day my boyfriend overheard me talking on the phone to somebody at work. He said: "You sound like a different person."'

Former blinkered bankers, those whose bubble had burst, felt like the City is almost designed to isolate you from society. Not everybody loses perspective, obviously: some successful bankers managed to keep both feet on the ground. It was striking how many of these were religious. They said that on entering their church, mosque or temple, their status and place in the financial hierarchy suddenly lost all relevance.

The million-dollar banker, too, spoke with almost clinical distance about bonuses. Relying on a bonus to make ends meet, he said, changes your psychology and affects your judgment. 'You will be tempted to tell yourself markets will go up – as such a bull market increases the chances of a new bonus.'

'Money comes and money goes but lifestyle comes and lifestyle stays,' echoed other neutrals, meaning that it is much easier to increase spending in tandem with a growing income than it is to cut back when your income is falling.

It sounds so logical, so self-evident that there is a standing expression for the trap of a rising income: *don't upgrade*. But now you are choosing a school for your children. Do you send them to the most expensive one? You can afford it, after all. Or do you go for the school that is not as good but a lot cheaper – so you can pay the fees even if you had to switch to a job paying considerably less? 'It is tough,' said a quant who was hoping to leave the sector in a few years. 'Your wife gets used to a standard of living, and I know that regardless of what I do next, I will always be working very hard. Why not stay on in this job that pays very well? You can see how these things may play out.'

Many juniors said they had actually been advised to increase their spending on clothes, cars and holidays. That is how you signal your motivation to your superiors. Saving up money implies you are hedging and keeping your options open. 'Watch your watch,' in the words of the German financial sociologist Bernd Ankenbrand: how can you realistically demand a high bonus with a £100 watch on your wrist?

A recruiter I would sometimes take out for lunch worked mostly with senior bankers. He emphasised that at many of the most prestigious investment banking desks your choice of car, home and second home, school, boat and holiday destination were crucial in projecting the right image. 'It's not like you have a choice,' he insisted. 'If you are with Goldman Sachs you can't go and live in some weird shack in Essex.'

•

I have found that many outsiders are deeply reluctant to accept that to an important degree the financial world isn't populated by people willfully doing evil but by conformists who have simply stopped asking questions about right and wrong. Things are going rather well for them and in their bubble they are exposed only to like-minded people.

Former investment banker Rainer Voss lived this life for years. 'You drive directly into the underground parking lot,' he says in his famous documentary *Master of the Universe*. 'You climb a few stairs to your workplace. And you really don't need to worry or care about the outside world. Your children attend the same nursery. You vacation in the same areas. Skiing in Gstaad or to the Seychelles or Mauritius. It's a closed system that leads you further away from reality.'

Did Voss have any friends outside that system? 'When you make $100,000 a month, you basically don't have common interests with your friends any more.'

In his memoirs, former chancellor of the exchequer Alistair Darling describes a discussion with a very high-ranking banker around the time of the crash. The gentlemen happened to know one another already and the banker expressed his outrage over plans by Labour to levy an extra tax on bonuses.

'I was rather taken aback by his anger,' Darling writes. His bonus amounted to around £1 million while the rest of the country would be facing deep cuts. 'What does your next-door neighbour say when you tell them you've got £1 million by way of a bonus?' Darling had asked.

'He doesn't mind,' the banker replied. What does your neighbour do, Darling enquired. 'He's a banker as well,' was the answer. 'And he earns more than me.'

To think that blinkered bankers will one day wake up and decide to change finance from within is wishful thinking. Indeed, it can be tempting to write blinkered bankers off entirely, even 'dehumanise' them: a privileged flock of selfish sheep.

But that was not how blinkered bankers were described in emails by readers who wrote in to say that sometimes they felt as if they had lost their daughter, son or best friend to the bank.

These readers used the blog to understand more of the world their now-remote loved ones had made their own. Some were prepared to meet me, for example a woman in her mid twenties from an Asian immigrant background who was dating a banker. When her interview was published, part of the comment thread exploded in angry contempt: what's next, the anonymous postman of a banker? The commenters had a point, but it seemed to strike a nerve with people in her position since no other interview from the blog has been shared more extensively on social media. It appeared many people recognised the type of behaviour she described.

Before turning to the final two types of bankers, having kept the most dangerous for last, here is her story:

'He always wanted this, to go into banking. And I never understood how this would impact my life. Over the summer it was still all right, his hours were between 9 a.m. and 7 p.m. I was like, OK, I can handle this. But things were already changing in him. He began to make jokes about how colleagues' wives spend their money. How the girlfriend of a colleague had to wait till 4 a.m. the next day for him to appear. He'd turn this into a joke. I began to realise: he is dropping hints.

'The first week his proper job started he was working till midnight every day. It's crazy how you adapt to that. These days when he finishes at 10 p.m. I think to myself: "Wow, that's really good."

'When I finished university I moved back with my parents. They don't know about us though they must suspect something now that I get phone calls at 1 a.m., 2 a.m. We used to talk on the phone every night before bed for at least 40 minutes to an hour. Now I just text him because I know there is no point in calling, he won't pick up. I go to bed and wake up the next day to find his text. 'Friday nights I stay over at the flat he recently moved in with a mate. It's an awful place; in his room there is just his bed and wardrobe. The kitchen is disgusting because it's never used. One time when I stayed there I had to wait till 3 a.m. for him to come home and back then he didn't even have a television or any internet. What I do now is I fill up my whole day and evening, because I don't want to sit in his flat waiting for him.

'When he comes home really late he's had six Red Bulls

and he'll want to talk. But I'm exhausted. I'm thinking, tomorrow morning we'll have a chat and a lie-in. But then he gets an email, saying: "Be in the office tomorrow by 9 a.m."

'I remember how one time back in our university days, we talked priorities. For me it was happiness, and being surrounded by loving people. For him that came second. The job was first. He is the sweetest man in the world. And I can see that this is what he wants to do, that this job is where his heart is.

'Sometimes he gets to leave the office by 8 p.m. He calls and I feel I have to cut my programme short because maybe we can spend an evening together, perhaps even go to a restaurant. When this happens I feel really stupid, leaving my friends and dropping everything for him. The power balance in our relationship has shifted completely.

'He is a great man and we had it really good in university. He's under a lot of pressure. His parents have financial difficulties and he is helping them pay their debts. He is very religious and he doesn't drink. This is not making things easier for him at the bank. In fact his parents have said that if he has to drink to get ahead at the bank, then that is OK. But he won't. Same dilemma with strip clubs. My position makes no sense, I know, but as long as we're not married, I'm OK if he has to go. But if we're married, then it's not acceptable.

'I was with him the day he got the phone call offering him the job. We were at a train station, he was so excited that he came running towards me and picked me up. People thought we were very strange, but we were just so excited – he had worked so hard and finally he had an offer.

'He is incredibly competitive. The other day we were talking about a friend of his who is also in finance, but with much better hours. I pointed that out to him and he went: "Oh no, he's with a shit bank, I don't want that."

'Is it making him happy? A little while ago we were having

dinner and he got a message that he had made a mistake. This threw him off completely. He couldn't stop fidgeting, wouldn't listen to me. The rest of the evening he was fretting about work.

'Everything has become provisional. When we plan something, he says, "But I may have to cancel." When we're out, there is always the chance of him getting called back into the office. He comes with terms and conditions. 'Oh God. You know, he tries really hard. But I told him very seriously: look, I don't like your job. I didn't choose to be in this situation. If I had wanted the bankers' lifestyle I would have gone into finance myself. I work in a shop. I live with my parents. I have huge student debts, a big overdraft . . . Now he has a really good salary, he looks smart – suddenly he holds all the cards in the relationship. 'He says things like, let me take you shopping. I don't want him to buy me presents to make up for the fact that he can't spend time with me. But this is how he talks now: I'll buy you something, I'll make it up to you.

'He is in mergers and acquisitions and when he talks about his job, I have all these acronyms thrown at me. Speak English, I want to scream. I met some of his colleagues and I dread meeting the others: "What do you do?," "I am in banking, and what do you?," "Well, I work in a shop." I have no credentials.

'These colleagues of his, they are like superpeople. Incredibly good-looking and intelligent and accomplished. I know what they have done to get there while I can't even be bothered to go for a run when it's cold out. I am not like them and I am fine with that but they are an intimidating group of people.

'Sadly, all they can talk about is work. Same with his flatmate who is with the same bank, but in a different division. You will not believe how boring and childish conversations between the two can be. Who works harder, how to get into the right jobs, how hard it is – they can go on all night. "My bank is better at M&A." "But my bank is great at . . ." and a few abbreviations fly across the room. One says, but you're not even a real trader. And then the other has to defend himself.

'It never stops. We may be together and then he's emailing India to get their guy there to finish something by 9 a.m. Sometimes he'll call the guy at home, in India, and make him go into the office. That's the pressure again. Some time ago I got a call and he said, "Oh my God, they're firing people right now." But he was allowed to stay.

'When he tells me what he does all day, I often think: I can do that. He'll be telling me that he spends at least half his time formatting documents; measuring the space between lines to make sure everything looks perfect. Presentation is so important in banking, apparently.

'Still it must be really hard, some of it. He has this colleague who cries all the time. She can't take the pressure. Apparently one managing director only wants to work with her, because of a particular skill she has. She'll be crying in the toilet and he'll cover for her, make up excuses why she isn't at her desk.

'I worry that I'm being too harsh on him. The thing is, I can't talk to my parents because they don't know he exists. My friends wouldn't understand, they are totally appalled when I tell them about his hours and what it means for us. I must find out what I actually feel. I don't know what I feel any more. Is it OK to rush through a dinner together because he has to go back into the office? When he doesn't call me, in the past I'd think: I'll have a go at him. Now I am making excuses why he didn't.

'Talk to him about it? That's the thing. I feel I can't even shout at him any more, can't tell him off. Because he has such a heavy job. In the old days when we fought it would last for hours. Three hours for the fight and then two hours silent treatment to get the point across. I don't do this any more because there's no time.

'So there we are. I travel an hour there and back on the tube just to see him, for maybe one hour. It's always me begging to see him: "What time do you finish?" I am getting into petty and ridiculous competitions with his family who are also claiming his time. During Christmas he had four days off and he couldn't even give me one.

'I would feel really awful if he lost his job for me. At the same time I have made these new friends over the past few months, and I can't even introduce them to him. They must think I have an imaginary boyfriend. I would like to introduce him to my sister. But he's never available before 11 p.m. and by that time my sister is asleep.'

'Last Saturday before he went into work I asked him if this job is what he wants to do with the rest of his life and he answered no. I was so surprised. But when I asked him what he wanted to do instead and how he saw his future, he told me he wasn't completely sure but that he would have to slog it out at the bank for a few years. After that he could practically go into anything.'

12

'Nobody Likes a Prophet of Doom'

On September 11, 2001, he was working as a trader at a top bank in London. As the first plane hit the towers many people were still thinking, or hoping, that it was an accident. He had a brainwave and called a good friend of his in New York: did he see any other planes or white trails in the sky? If not, the airspace over New York had been closed, meaning the authorities were treating this as a terrorist attack. The sky was blue and empty so as soon as he could he started selling stocks in insurance companies, in airliners . . . Never in his life had he worked so hard as he did on that day and never did he make his bank so much money. The London markets were closing, he did his digital paperwork and only then did it occur to him that he knew people in the Twin Towers. 'I had friends were working there,' he said, almost indignantly. 'Until that point I had not thought of them, not for a second.'

Alongside neutrals, teeth grinders, Masters of the Universe and blinkered bankers, I found in the City two more groups of people. As with the blinkered bankers, both groups could be studied only indirectly, through people who work with them or as interviewees who claimed they used to have been one.

The first group might be called the delusional bankers, as they have lost touch not only with the rest of society but also with reality. The trader quoted above said he had spent years in a 'tunnel' of work addiction. That evening of September 11 had been a turning point. 'Not that I resigned the next day or anything dramatic like that. But something had changed in me.' Some time later he did leave his bank and switched careers.

When delusional bankers talked about the first few years at their bank, most sounded like classic Masters of the Universe: analytically intelligent, hyper-competitive and bursting with an attitude for which the egalitarian Dutch have a special term: *geldingsdrang*, or the urge to impress others. Masters of the Universe, however, know what they are doing; they are playing the status game, and to do so they have internalised a particular perspective and will defend it vigorously with others – in fact, they will relish the chance to do so. By contrast, delusional bankers exist in a tunnel; they have lost touch with reality. They are addicted to their work, they don't acknowledge there is a problem and there is no longer a coherent perspective underpinning their views.

Then these bankers burn out.

As a senior human resources officer with ABN Amro, Kilian Wawoe had regularly dealt with delusional bankers. Outsiders ask me when bankers ever have enough, he said. But for some it is not about the money. 'It's a highly addictive status game. Pay marks your status in the organisation. This is why there is no saturation point.'

'Investment bankers think of themselves as hyper individualists,' said a woman who insisted I release no further details about her. 'Yet when working so hard and such long hours we completely forget ourselves. Which is the opposite of individualism.'

For years she had done little else other than working, working and working. When she did have free time she went on intensive, adventurous holidays or ran half marathons to raise funds for charities. Everything was a riveting and all-absorbing competition with colleagues: always optimising and pushing yourself further, finding your limits and then transcending them.

We are doing it to ourselves, she emphasised. 'How do you forget yourself? Management give you a profits and and loss target for the year. You say, guys, this number is completely unrealistic. At the same time you feel the pull of the challenge; can you do it, against all odds? What happens is that since you accepted the game, you feel you are yourself to blame when you don't hit the target. Over time your target for the year comes to define who you are. What you want in life is now whatever brings you closer to that target. You forget to ask yourself: what do I want to achieve with my life?'

After a very serious mental breakdown she had quit, taken the time to recover before deciding to train as a therapist and coach. She kept on stressing how grateful she was for all the experiences at her bank, the opportunities she had been given and the wonderfully inspiring colleagues she had learnt so much from. But she had been in a bad place, when she resigned, physically as well as mentally. 'You have to assume this persona without emotions. I found myself crying in the loo so many times. That's the only place where you can be a human being: in the loo. The crying never lasts long. You let go and reassume your persona. Because you have to go back in.'

Interviews with former or recovering delusional bankers had the atmosphere of a therapy session: I'm told it helps to reach out and talk about this. Or: 'I want to shake others out of their delusions.' And: 'When I started seeing a therapist for a while I discovered that half his client base, many at the top, were in finance. All had been brainwashed into thinking that being ill meant weakness. That having emotions were a sign of weakness. When I read the interviews on your blog, I could tell which ones had been successfully brainwashed, and which ones hadn't.'

A dealmaker who had spent two decades taking companies public quoted Larkin's haunting image: 'fulfilment's desolate attic.' 'I have read athletes' accounts in which they describe standing on the podium after they won, feeling nothing at all.' That was what it had been like for him after each bonus – which in his final years could easily come to £1 million. Having taken advantage of the same conflicts of interest that made the dot-com scandal possible, he eventually fell into a depression and resigned. Investment banking 'is a trap, a game and an addiction.

The reward is big, but uncertain, which makes it exciting and keeps you coming back for more. Once the money starts flowing it's very, very hard to take yourself away from it. There are these people queuing up behind you, eyeing your job. Also there is the emptiness that comes with addiction.'

The big danger is that you outsource your existential questions to the bank, said those who felt they had spent years living an illusion. You hit your target so your life must be a success.

'My flatmate is in finance too,' said a junior dealmaker who had just quit his job after two years with his bank. 'I've seen him coming home crying, from exhaustion, from something that happened to him. Why are we doing this to ourselves? My sense is that the majority of the people in finance have an urge to prove themselves. And banks offer a platform where they can do so. I feel there's a particular kind of insecurity to many bankers, a form of neediness and a deep desire to compensate for something. The absence of love, perhaps?'

Many people in banking try to project an image of perfection, he had found. 'Banks play to that, trying to make you look perfect and feel invulnerable. It's very easy to get hooked into that life, to become addicted to work and the money. I am sure it would have happened to me, had I done this for too long.'

When doing research for the Gordon Gekko character in the famous film *Wall Street*, scriptwriter Stanley Weiser spoke to a great number of top financial workers. In an interview on the DVD Weiser echoes the idea of finance as an existential trap for those with addictive personalities: 'The Gekkos of the world are people who have a complete inability to process the reality of . . . of death. It's the game, the energy, the momentum of continuing to play the game . . .'

The first few times I heard about delusional bankers I thought, well, that's too bad but every profession must have vulnerable people who develop an unhealthy addiction to their jobs.

However, the world of finance is not an industry like any other and a handful of delusional people can cause immense damage. In the so-called Libor and FX scandals, traders at big banks and brokerages manipulated crucial interest and currency rates for their own gain over years and years. This was illegal and the traders must have known this, as they must have known that all their internal communication was being recorded and archived – in case of misunderstandings or disputes, the middle office must be able to play back what was said between the bank and the client.

And yet, after successfully manipulating a particular rate they exchanged self-congratulatory emails or chat massages completely openly. A typical message ran: 'Dude. I owe you big time! Come over one day after work and I'm opening a bottle of Bollinger.' One trader asked another how it could be so easy to make money, while the messaging groups where they exchanged all this were given names like 'the cartel,' 'the mafia or 'the bandits' club.'

You might say: what utter shamelessness. And going over these messages you do not feel that these traders lived in fear of their risk and compliance department. But above all these emails and chat messages are completely irrational: what sane criminal would congratulate his mates in public on the latest robbery?

Only when you realise these traders were living in a cloud of self-delusion do their actions make sense.

The Libor and FX scandals were scandals in the true sense of the word but the crash is of course the most important and urgent reason to closely study self-delusion among bankers. Which brings me to what must be the most terrifying interview of all.

We met in a Starbucks somewhere in central London. He was an inconspicuously dressed man, of medium build, in his late forties. He had been very high up in treasury at a bank that had to be saved after it collapsed under the risks it had taken. This was a commercial bank and the practices that went so disastrously wrong are now banned. That is not what is scary about the interview, though. It is the mentality he describes.

I started out by asking what outsiders fail to understand about the City and he said it was how you get sucked into the corporate culture. 'Bankers work in teams, and the ethic there is: you are with us or you're against us. Speaking out makes you vulnerable. If you have a guilty secret hidden somewhere, they'll find it and expose you. You know that if you take something public, they'll find a way of getting back at you. They won't sack you right away but when there's a new round of redundancies.' This is why the only people to blow the whistle are those with very high morals, and those who are simply beyond caring. Before the crash his bank was taking so much risk the money came flooding in, bringing his pay to between a quarter and half a million a year. 'We were on top of the world. Risk produces profits, profits lead to a higher share price, and executive pay was linked to that. It was so fucking easy to manipulate the share price; simply take some more risk.'

He travelled around the world and had tickets to every major sporting event. 'Everyone is nice to you because you represent a chance for them to make money. It becomes very tempting to think that actually all these people like you for who you are.'

Internally he did stress the risks the bank was taking. But you have to understand: 'Nobody likes a prophet of doom.' He also remembered thinking, 'What the hell, it's not my money, is it? I suppose that's why I could cope with the stress reasonably well. I always saw it as a bit of a laugh. I had gathered this band of anti-establishment people around me and we would mock the seriousness of the banking world.'

For the financial sector to ever improve, he said, 'you'd have to untangle the inherent tendency to amorality. And that tendency is embedded in the system. Regulation to keep the City in check? Don't hold your breath. No matter what rules you put in place, they'll always find ways around it. It's like the Prohibition.'

In an amoral environment like that, he went on, right and wrong became 'blurry' and hard to define. 'If you shaft people and get a very good deal, that's considered the greatest thing there is. What I mean is that in business when you deliberately, consciously make money out of someone, that's what it's all about, isn't it? Excessive profitability is deemed cause for promotion. Drug companies try to get you to take as many medicines as they can, while thinking of themselves as being in the business of curing disease.'

Having said that, he continued, he did think the City fundamentally differed from other business sectors and the civil service. 'I am sure the things we're talking about are happening there, too. What makes the City so special is that historically the sector has been very close together. There are all these pubs and bars close by where you can meet discreetly. It becomes a huge playground, a social network at very close proximity. You can bond very easily, and become bonded to like-minded people. Colleagues become buddies. Throw in the alcohol and the client entertainment and you get an explosive mix. Boundaries are crossed very easily, leading to massive conflicts of interest. Brokers and traders are friends, but one also gives business to the other. "I'll get tickets for rugby for you if you do that trade with me" – that sort of thing happens very easily.'

Back then he never thought he was stressed because being successful in finance requires you to hide your anxiety. First from others and over time, from yourself. What's more, he said, 'There just wasn't any time for self-reflection. I ended up drinking huge amounts. Alcohol is a quick mood changer; it stops you from thinking and dulls you down. Not that I was aware of that at the time.'

I remained quiet, waiting for him to break the silence. This isn't just due to the bonus culture, he said in a tone that suggested he had thought about this a lot. 'This is about tribal bonding, about belonging and sticking with your mates. Your sense of worth begins to be formed by what you do. It is often the first question people ask you, right? What do you do? In that time, when I answered that question, I was a superstar.'

Going public with something he believed to be wrong would have meant placing himself 'in one stroke' outside of that world. 'It's not just your job. It's your identity.'

And then you decided to quit? 'There was no tipping point and it took me a long time to untangle myself. There were a trillion reasons. A general feeling of malaise, corporate and personal. There was fear, absolutely: the fear of fucking something up big time. Because I wasn't taking things seriously I wasn't doing everything I could to prevent that. And that made me afraid. Then the personal malaise: what was I becoming? My marriage was in trouble.'

The birds singing, mucking about with the kids . . . when you're working so hard, he said, you just don't expose yourself to these things and over time you forget they exist. He knew now that he had become 'not a nice person. The kindness you show to your parents . . . I stopped doing that. And I wasn't aware that I had stopped doing that. I had my mates. They were like me. I was like them.'

It's weird how your perspective changes once you are out, he said. Therapy helped him find his feet again. He admitted that having earnt so much money he was very lucky to be saved from financial trauma. Friends in the bank had asked him: 'Why would you leave? Just stay around, get paid well, do nothing.'

He couldn't. 'It had become existential. What's this all for? Am I really enjoying this?'

So did he have regrets? He took a deep breath. 'I am not going to give this massive apology – well, maybe I should? If I am sorry for anything, it's for what I became in those years. God, I am beginning to sound incredibly selfish.'

Another silence. 'Anybody can get out. You might say I was weak for jumping out. You might say I was strong in making this point. What would I say to somebody reading this who is in the position I was in for a long time? Look in the mirror and ask yourself: "Is the City turning me into a nasty person?" Then again, since people lose the ability for self-reflection, I wonder if anybody would look in that mirror.'

This was the interview that pushed me from anger directly

into despair and as I was writing up my notes I caught myself thinking a few times: please, don't let this be true.

It might be possible to reform the incentive structure in banks so that bankers are no longer rewarded for lying to their superiors, to the middle office, to accountants, to credit rating agencies, to the regulator and to their clients. 'Long-term greedy' is the insiders' term for such a system without perverse incentives; as a banker you make money *with* your bank and your clients, rather than at their expense.

But the point is that delusional bankers have by definition stopped responding rationally to incentives. Following the Libor case, the United Kingdom adopted a law that allows for the prosecution of bankers who can be proven to have taken excessive risk. It sounds like the sort of measure we need except that one must ask: would this have stopped the treasurer above from embarking on his bank's financial death spiral?

The treasurer was not so much lying to others as to himself. How do you reach someone living in the mist of self-delusion and addiction?

This is why financial activists call for the radical shrinkage and simplification of banks. They believe that we should not waste energy on financial reform that aims to prevent another bank from collapsing. Future defaults are inevitable since there will always be incompetent and irrational people and sooner or later a bank will fall into their hands. The aim must be to organise the world of finance in such a way that a collapsing bank cannot drag down the world economy with it. In a soundbite: too big to fail is too big to exist.

•

If the Masters of the Universe, blinkered and delusional bankers form the human powder keg at the heart of today's financial sector, the final type, then, would be the fuse. This is the group that comes closest to the proverbial evil bankers: creeps who know exactly what they are doing. Except that these 'cold fish,' as I have come to call them, were not creepy at all. They are extremely calculating and seek to eliminate all emotions from their decision-making. Since cold fish reduce everything to a transaction they were impossible to interview. If you merely look to maximise your own 'utility' there is simply no reason to risk your job to give an interview that in the best case is so well anonymised that nobody will ever know it was you.

As with the blinkered and delusional bankers I had to rely on indirect channels, such as interviewees who admitted they once thought like a cold fish. I managed to interview 'active' cold fish only a handful of times. One of these was a trader at a megabank with literary ambitions. He spoke to me because he wanted the *Guardian* website to hyperlink his anonymous blog.

He was a so-called prop trader, which meant, in his words, using the bank's own money to make more money for the bank. A typical day for him started in the middle of the night, since 'his' emerging market was at the other side of the globe.

'I work from two principles,' he said. 'You need to be dispassionate about your trade, to control your internal hurdles that may attach you to it emotionally. Second, you need to have specific knowledge of the asset you're trading. You must have contacts in the asset's country that can supply you with information that is open to anyone else – otherwise it's insider trading – but that is still extremely valuable.'

I asked for examples and he mentioned the quality of the management of the company whose shares he was contemplating buying as the best guideline. Next you are going to look at the country's economy that company is working in, the political environment, the regulatory environment. 'That's how you build a view on an investment and may decide to trade in it.'

He characterised prop trading as 'one huge lesson in humility' and the best traders are like Buddhists: in complete control of their emotions and never falling prey to fear when things are difficult or to greed when the market does better than expected. Fear and greed entrap so many people, he said. 'No matter what's whirling in my mind, follow the argument' on the basis of which you decided to trade a particular asset in the first place.

For Master of the Universe types he had nothing but scorn, because as a trader you should let nothing impact your ego.

This prop trader had many characteristics of a cold fish but the true archetype was the quant I met who working in high frequency trading. He was thinking about a career as a writer and in order to start building a network he had sought me out. There was something in it for him and he was open about that.

Almost the entire interview was taken up by his explanation of high frequency trading and this elicited so many comments on the blog that I wanted to give him the right of reply. So we met again and I put it to him that many readers were asking how he could live with himself.

That's right, he answered. 'I couldn't show the portrait to anyone at work, as they don't know I am doing this. But I sent it to my parents and siblings. They said two things: everybody hates you. And we finally have some idea what your job is.'

What had infuriated readers more than anything was that they saw no value to society in high frequency trading, particularly the 'prop' form that the quant was working in. Meanwhile readers could see that the scope for abuse and catastrophic errors was huge.

'Look, I am not ashamed of what I do,' he said with a perfectly calm and pleasant smile. 'Others may choose to devote their programming skills to making the NHS work better. If that's their choice, I'm happy for them. It's everyone's free choice and I made mine in working in this field. Capitalism means trading on markets, that's what our programme does. We are simply the extreme and fastest version of the principle of trading. What does a second-hand car salesman contribute to society? He doesn't improve on the car, he is simply making money from the difference between what sellers and buyers are prepared to pay.'

What I do for a living is legal, period. That is the cold fish mentality and this turns morality into a private matter, or rather one of the options available to human beings – the way some choose to give money to a charity, or to follow an extra two-credit point course in ethics. Or not.

All other attempts to debate what is right and wrong hit a brick wall for this type of banker. The big difference between cold fish and neutrals is that neutrals will maintain an ethical sense, voluntarily abstaining from activities they consider im-moral. By contrast, a cold fish believes the law defines what is acceptable. If something is legally permissible – even if it is at the very fringes of legality – then what's the problem?

The quant demonstrated this attitude clearly. Any ques-tions about ethical responsibility were returned to me with a faintly amused expression: who did I think I was? A moralist? A paternalist?

The quant seemed like a regular kind of guy – the opposite of immoral. He simply applied the amoral principles of his sec-tor to his own life. Here again, 'greed' as an all-encompassing explanation for his motives seemed to fall short. Indeed, he was hoping in a few years' time to have enough money and time to become a writer. 'I would like to go back to university. I have become very interested in the humanities and philosophy.'

Nobody taught me more about cold fish bankers than a recruiter I would sometimes take out for a drink. While he seemed like a neutral himself, many of the bankers he was working with fitted the cold fish category. So how can they live with themselves?

'Many of my clients simply don't seem to care a whole lot about what the general public think. These are extremely well-educated and multilingual professionals. Many are in mixed marriages with kids who have lived on two or three continents. These people don't belong anywhere and don't feel beholden to any national project. They want to pay as little in tax as they can, and they want to be safe. That's it. Rule of law is very important for them. 'My clients are not bad people. They are people who no longer think in terms of good and evil. Professionals.'

•

Two hundred interviews may feel like a gigantic task when you are conducting them but taken together the interviewees comprise less than 0.1 per cent of the quarter of a million employees in the City. No doubt there are more types of bankers and banking staff to be found but for this project the cold fish seemed to close the circle.

Somewhere in the vast archipelago that the megabank has become, a maths genius with the mindset of a cold fish dreams up a highly innovative complex financial product. The regulator finds it extremely difficult to judge the hidden risks and unintended knock-on effects. The product is very lucrative, the competition is building them too, and top management think: 'As long as the music is playing, you've got to get up and dance.' Masters of the Universe, blinkered and delusional bankers start selling the product as widely as they can. The middle office is intimidated or charmed into submission or grinds its teeth as it looks the other way, while the neutrals remain aloof . . .

That is how another crash can happen, at least according

to a cold fish who had recently quit his job. Whenever I heard angry outsiders dismissing bankers as monsters I'd send them a link to this interview. And if somebody declared the problems in the world of finance to be solved, I'd do the same.

He was around 35 years old and after his degree in maths had gone to work for a top bank as a structurer, inventing and building complex financial products. There are lots of different structurers and his area was that of the equity derivatives, the same field as former Goldman Sachs banker Greg Smith.

It was like the story of Dr Faustus, he said over a flat white coffee. 'You sell your soul to the devil. I sold my soul for worldly riches. The price the devil demanded was my moral bankruptcy. For a long time I was OK with that, until I wasn't. What triggered this change of heart? There was not one particular moment. You have to look at yourself in the mirror every morning. I imagined a future son or daughter asking me, Daddy, what do you do for a living? What was I going to say? "Well, sweetie, Daddy rips clients off?"'

He began to wonder what people would say at his funeral speech. 'I am an atheist, you know, I believe that this life is it.'

He started talking about caveat emptor and deceiving clients without breaking a single law or rule.

'There are smaller players who basically have no idea what they're doing. Some small Spanish savings bank perhaps or some municipality in Sweden. What got to me after a while is how I'd be lying in the faces of these less sophisticated parties.' He had a working-class background and his family was paying premiums into the kind of pension funds he was going after. 'I'd be thinking, wow, this is my parents' pension money down the drain.'

As a student he had been 'a real neoliberal. I read Ayn Rand, absorbed the idea that markets were great, that there was nothing else that worked. Then over time, I got more critical.'

These days he had lost much of that optimism and no longer thought that 'the market' can work by itself. In fact he believed regulators needed to become 'much, much firmer. I have been thinking about joining them, in fact. My sense is that regulators have good intentions, but the complexity of the industry makes it very difficult. And there's the lobbying.'

He took a sip of his flat white and pointed out that he was still pro-free market, 'no mistake about that.' Companies need to raise money to invest, he said, to innovate and to expand. Ordinary people need returns on their savings so at some point they can retire. 'This should be the raison d'être for the financial sector. But by now the sector has grown so much in size and complexity . . . And as a result the opportunities to abuse the system have multiplied by many times. Many times.'

The crash of 2008 has 'crippled' the western world, he said, and the consequences will be with us for another ten years, at least. 'It is really big, and something like that can happen again. I'm sure that in four or five years, some smart structurer will find a clever way to get around this regulation, and God knows what will happen then.'

His career in finance lasted over ten years, and by the end he was making around £800,000 a year. He had saved it all and had never gone for the expensive car and so on. As a result he would never have to work again in his life. He could have stayed with his bank for many more years but had chosen not to – another indication that 'greed' is not the driver, or the only driver.

It's strange, he said after a short silence. 'Bankers are so smart, yet they get this thing wrong. They spend their lives in an office when the only truly valuable thing in life is time. It is the only thing that is not replenishable. You can always make more money, but you can never get more time. Maybe it's because death is such a taboo in our society; people live in this illusion that their life will go on forever. Or maybe they are afraid of the time, if they'd take it, if they'd stop working those insane hours.'

After quitting his job he had spent a lot of time thinking and found great appeal in stoicism. 'No matter how much stuff you have, you will always get used to it and want more. So it's much smarter to imagine you have much less, and then enjoy what you have. Under the shower this morning I imagined what my life would be like without running hot water. That's reality for 5 billion other people on this planet. I ended up thoroughly enjoying my shower, deeply grateful.'

He emphasised once more that he was not complaining. 'I have no respect for people in finance who complain. They have a choice to do this. If you are some poor guy in some war-torn country, living off $2 a day, then you can complain. Then you can't choose.'

I asked if he had ever considered giving back the money he made? He took his time to consider. 'Well, I am morally ambiguous about that. Everyone is greedy; look at the average person in the west. When you buy a T-shirt for £3, do you think of the guy in Bangladesh who made it, working 12 hours a day for a shit salary?'

In the first world we all live at the expense of the other 5 billion. 'So if I am to give back my earnings, we should all do so. How did the Bible express that? He who is without sin cast the first stone.'

Many readers will explode at this, I suggested. He nodded gravely: 'Every era has seen its scapegoats, and today it's the bankers. I can live with that stigma.'

13

The Empty Cockpit

The American writer Ron Rosenbaum has remarked that deep down most journalists are Freudians. Like the founder of psychoanalysis, journalists believe that the most important things in the world are kept hidden and need to be dug up, be it in therapy or through investigation. Then journalists think, like Freud did, that bringing those hidden and shocking facts to the surface and exposing them leads to improvement.

The classical model is Watergate. President spies on his opponents. Journalists reveal this. President steps down. The system has corrected itself.

It is a fine theory, but with global finance things do not seem to work this way. The conflicts of interest and perverse incentives pervading the sector were exposed long ago, if only by those countless parliamentary investigations that took place after the crash. Recently Andrew Haldane told the German magazine *Der Spiegel* that the balances of the big banks are 'the blackest of black holes.' Haldane is the number two of the English central bank with responsibility for the stability of the financial sector as a whole. He says out loud that he can't possibly have an idea of what the banks have on their books. And?

Nothing happens.

This puts journalists and other commentators in a confus-
ing position. We believe that we must go out to find 'news': important stories and facts that nobody knows about. But when
it comes to global finance the most startling news isn't news at
all; important facts have been known for a long time among
insiders. The problem goes much deeper: the sector has become
immune to exposure.

For journalists this state of affairs means, I think, that we
must try to make the world of finance accessible to outsiders.
More people need to understand how dangerous the global financial sector still is, how in 2008 it took us to the brink and
that the deeper causes of that near-catastrophe have not been
tackled.

Those who now expect this final chapter to present a master
plan, however, are fooling themselves. Designing a new architecture for global finance far outstrips the abilities of one individual, even more so because the problems and dysfunctionality
are not limited to the banks. Many hedge funds, for example,
have been found to engage in the same kind of highly lucrative, technically legal activities with immoral consequences as
banks, from speculating against complex financial products to
blackmailing countries such as Argentina and Greece.

Even more fundamental is the current financial and monetary system, which is creating one 'bubble' after another. With
the help of clever financial products, governments and individuals extract money from those bubbles ('cash in on the increase
in your home's value'). This encourages consumer spending,
which goes on to count towards economic 'growth.' That increase in GDP is then used to justify even more borrowing and
credit creation. And so the bubble continues to grow.

All the signs are pointing to the need for a complete overhaul of our financial and monetary system — not repairs or a

major clean-up but a completely new DNA.

Such a master plan is not going to be easy to administer, but the first step is to be clear about the nature of the problem. One thing I believe does *not* help is to reduce the problems with global finance down to individual character flaws. Yes, there is a lot of greed in the City, as there is elsewhere. But if you blame all the scandals as well as the crash on individuals you imply that the system itself is fine, all we need to do is to smoke out the crooks: the greedy gambling addicts, the coke-snorters, the psychopaths . . .

Human beings are not sheep and they always have at least some scope for choice; hence the differences in culture between banks. Still, human behaviour is largely determined by incentives and in the current set-up these are sending individual bankers, desks or divisions within banks – as well as the banks themselves – in the wrong direction.

I am convinced that were we to pack off the entire City to a desert island and replace them a quarter of a million new people, we would see in no time the same kind of abuse and dysfunctionality. The problem is the system and rather than angrily blaming individual bankers for acting on their perverse incentives we should put our energy into removing those incentives.

This requires better laws and it is not at all difficult to see the four changes those laws should bring. First of all, banks must be chopped up into units so that they are no longer too big or too complex to fail – this would mean that they can no longer blackmail us. Banks should not have activities under one roof that create conflicts of interest, be it between trading, asset management and deal making or between consumer banking on the one hand and riskier investment banking on the other. Third, banks should not be allowed to build, sell or own overly complex financial products, so clients can comprehend what they buy and investors can understand a bank's balance sheet. Finally, the bonus should land on the same head as the 'malus,' meaning nobody should have more reason to lie awake at night worrying over the risks to the bank's capital or reputation than the bankers taking those risks.

It is not rocket science, and you would expect all major political parties in all the western democracies to have come out by now with their vision of a stable and productive financial sector. Either a coherent argument why they believe the status quo is safe and fair, or a point on the horizon: this is what we believe the financial sector should look like and this is our road-map to get there.

That is how democracy works, in theory at least, and this is why journalists are Freudians: we expose what is going wrong so voters can elect the politicians with the most convincing plans to fix the mess.

Except that after 2008 things did not work out that way. In the two and a half years that the blog ran, readers left at least 10,000 comments. Not a single person wrote: 'Oh, if only the Labour party were in power because then . . .'

This was not due to apathy, I think. It was rather a realistic appraisal that when it comes to financial overhaul, it does not really matter whether Labour or the Conservatives are in power. As it makes no real difference whether in Germany the Social Democrats are in or out of the coalition, if the Republicans or the Democrats hold power in the United States, or France has a government of the left or the right.

Why have western democracies failed to articulate solutions for one of the most urgent issues of our times – let alone competing visions that offer voters a choice?

In political parties there must be a lot of Master of the Universe types for whom politics is all a game anyway. There are no doubt cold fish, too, who have gone into politics for a calculated period of time in order to acquire status, privileges and contacts. As there will be blinkered politicians living in a bubble.

However, I know from experience that you will find in political parties 'neutrals' as well: people with a very sharp eye for what is going wrong and what needs to change. The problem is that those neutrals go on to say: what is the use if I go after the financial sector on my own? What do you think will happen to my position within the party? Or to my party?

What's more, neutrals will say: look at what is awaiting political parties and individual politicians who decide to stay within the lines drawn for them by the financial sector. In America, France and the UK, the law allows banks and bankers to buy political power – known in another fine example of obscuring language as 'campaign donations' rather than 'corruption.'

Then there is the immense financial lobby and a phenomenally lucrative 'speaker circuit.' After their time in office as minister of finance and foreign affairs, respectively, Timothy Geithner and Hillary Clinton gave a number of speeches at Goldman Sachs for which they were paid $200,000. Apiece.

That is nice work if you can get it and this is even truer of the so-called 'second careers.' Former Labour Prime Minister Tony Blair is not alone in making vastly more money as 'adviser' to a megabank than he was earning when serving his country. German central bank president Axel Weber went on to lead the Swiss megabank UBS while top American policy-makers such as Robert Rubin and Lawrence Summer spent one part of their career in public office deregulating the financial industry, another part working in that same financial sector.

Across the West, politics and public office are changing from being a countervailing power to the world of finance, to becoming a springboard for individuals to move into that world.

So is it all due to – perfectly legal – corruption? The idea that the financial sector has 'bought' politicians' apathy before 2008 implies that top management in banks realised what a mess they were creating. It implies that top management also realised that politicians realised this, prompting the former to buy the latter's silence.

It seems more likely that over the past decades, mainstream political parties and politicians as well as regulators have come to identify themselves with the financial sector and the people in it. The term here is 'capture,' a form of cognitive herd behaviour popularised by the economist and former *Financial Times* columnist Willem Buiter. With corruption you are given money to do something you would not have done otherwise. Capture is more subtle and no longer requires the transfer of funds since the politician, academic or regulator has started to believe that the world works in the way that bankers say it does.

At this point I would have loved to quote from a magnum opus by Willem Buiter in which he examines the phenomenon of capture in historical and comparative perspective. Sadly that standard work remains to be written. Willem Buiter no longer works in academia and journalism. He has moved to the megabank Citigroup.

There is another important reason for the political impasse before and after 2008. Political parties, too, have teeth grinders in their ranks, with one difference: they are not so much concerned about their job as they are for their country. Their argument typically runs like this: 'OK, let us assume our country takes on its financial sector. In that case our banks and financial firms simply move elsewhere, meaning we will have lost our voice in international forums. Meanwhile, globally, nothing has changed.'

The fact is that megabanks and huge financial institutions operate globally, say politicians of this school, while politics and regulations are organised nationally or at best in continents or blocks. Financial institutions can play off countries and blocks of countries against each other and this they do, shamelessly.

This political powerlessness in the face of global finance is infuriating and raises the question of whether globalisation is even compatible with national democracy. How are we to bring the global financial sector under control, without a legitimate global government? And if you believe such a global government to be unfeasible or undesirable, does this not imply that globally operating financial institutions of a size and power that dwarfs national governments are untenable, too?

This is the empty cockpit.

•

Journalists are meant to be happy when the story they have immersed themselves in proves to be bigger, more spectacular and relevant than expected. The conflicts of interest and perverse incentives in the heart of global finance will continue to produce lots of copy for front-page articles but this fails to make me celebrate. Yes, I am a writer keen for success. But I am also a citizen of my society. Thinking of how dangerous and explosively unstable the global financial sector has become, and how deeply embedded, I feel something close to nausea. How is this ever going to be put right, or at least brought back under control?

Radically higher capital buffers would immediately make the banks far safer but even this relatively simple measure has been sabotaged successfully by the global banking lobby. Even worse, no credible alternative to the financial status quo has been developed in the case of the next crash. That crash will therefore be 'won' by the global financial sector again, meaning the rest of us will have to pay up once more before seeing the system being restarted the way it was after 2008 – assuming it will be possible to resurrect it in the first place.

In this respect it might be better to speak of the 'near-crash of 2008.' After all, the real disaster was averted – with lots of luck and money.

That is where we are, seven years after Lehman. The City, meanwhile, hasn't been sitting on its hands. It is the job of a whole sector of bankers to get individuals, companies and governments across the UK and the rest of Europe to borrow as much money as possible. Other bankers sell those individuals, companies and governments complex financial instruments that help obscure those debts from view, while other bankers sell on the debts in order to make yet more borrowing possible for their bank. When the next bubble bursts another group of bankers come forward with proposals to use a series of privatisations to plug the holes in the state budget.

The United Kingdom and the rest of Europe are being re-shaped in the image of the City and this is no conspiracy but a simple projection of existing incentives into the future. The most driven bankers consider their jobs a status game. That game consists of lending money, packing and selling on debts, and privatisations. The more business they do, the higher those bankers will rise in the league tables they have constructed their identities around. What a heartless place global finance has become – and more generally the globalised corporate world. As one reader put in an email: 'Where all love has disappeared, all that remains is the will to win.'

There is a social Darwinist undertone running through the cult of meritocracy that underpins today's global financial sector which any credible alternative will have to confront head on. The recruiter who taught me so much about 'cold fish' bankers hit on some very painful truths, at least for those of us with a progressive outlook on life. I had told him that his clients sounded almost like the crew of 'Spaceship Finance.' Their vessel happens to have landed in London for now, but it could take off any time. He agreed: 'A highly educated professional in the City of London has much more in common with a peer in Hong Kong, New York City or Rio de Janeiro, than with a monolingual, mono-cultural teacher or nurse somewhere up in Birmingham or Manchester. Solidarity for the new global elite is not geography-based or tied up with a state.'

Knowing this was for the progressive *Guardian*, the recruiter added mischievously: 'This is where the left seems lost. It insists on solidarity across the nation, with higher tax rates for rich people to help their less fortunate countrymen. But this solidarity is predicated on a sense of national belonging, to which the left is allergic; national identity comes with chauvinism and nationalism, and creepy right-wing supremacists. It's quite ironic how postmodernists and many contemporary social thinkers on the left will tell you that all sense of belonging is a construct, tradition is invented and nations are simply fantasies or imagined communities. Well, the global financial elite agrees.'

•

'I no longer feel safe,' said a friend after reading an earlier version of this book and I have asked myself if I should publish this book at all. What is the point of leaving one's readers in powerless fear and outrage?

But the world of finance is not some far-away land that can be safely ignored. If money is to society what blood is to the body then the financial sector is the heart; pump too much or too little and the body suffers, interrupt the pumping altogether – even for a brief period – and the body may never recover.

Ignorance, denial or apathy is simply not an option when

it comes to a problem of this magnitude and urgency. Before coming to the City I lived and worked for many years in Egypt. That is a dictatorship where citizens have no options in the face of a crisis except resignation or armed resistance. Popular uprisings exhaust themselves or are put down and the opposition is either in jail, exiled or in hiding.

That is how powerless citizens are in a dictatorship. However, the West has developed a political system that can pull itself up by its own bootstraps. Cynicism about the current crop of mainstream political leaders seems entirely justified. If they were planning to take on the power of global finance politics in a serious way they would have told us by now.

To write off politics, however, seems the dumbest thing we could do. A democratic system is and remains the best opportunity for ordinary citizens to wrest power back from global finance through peaceful means. It is also the best opportunity for the sector itself to reform, before it is too late.

A transformation of this kind is an immense task. On the other hand, has the West not reinvented itself with great success before in the past 200 years? The abolition of slavery and the liberation of women demanded far greater and deeper changes than are now required with finance.

Nobody is helped more by cynicism about politics than cynical politicians.

Methodology

The laws and conventions of journalism demand verifiable information and attributed quotes. This is for very good reasons but when it comes to finance and the City these rules render investigative research effectively impossible. Quoting a banker in the City turns him or her automatically into an ex-banker while 'authorised' interviews in the presence of PR officers are extremely unlikely to lead to revelations and insights.

Any researcher looking into finance has to find a way around this code of silence and the culture of fear. The solution in this book has been to offer sources full anonymity but it is important to emphasise that this method comes at a cost. Nearly every interviewee made a point of stressing how different the corporate culture in one bank or division in a bank can be from another. The problem was that interviewees could not discuss these differences without naming these banks and thereby putting their anonymity at risk.

About this project: from the summer of 2011 till the early autumn of 2013 I met with around 200 people who work or recently worked in the City. Most I would see only once, others a few times and some more than tenfold. A little under 100 interviews appeared online on the *Guardian* blog (www. guardiannews.com/jlbankingblog) where they can still be read. Those who do so will see that some of the quotes have been lightly edited for readability. They will also discover that the chronology in which the interviews are published does not always tally with the 'learning curve' as related in this book. The reason is that while, say, interviewee number 19 was the first to make a particular observation, it was interviewee 106 who put the same thing far more powerfully. In those cases I have always used the best available quotes and anecdotes. A number of interviewees appear throughout the book. In order not to bury the reader in long and repetitive job descriptions these interviewees are accompanied by a few words summarising the relevant element in their background: 'a compliance officer,' 'a veteran with 10 years of experience in internal controls.'

A sector as huge, diverse and complex as that of finance, with so much jargon and partly overlapping terminology, is impossible to make accessible to outsiders without cutting corners. In other words, I have had to simplify things drastically. The definition of 'commercial banking' is more complex and nuanced than chapter two says it is and whereas I am calling Goldman Sachs a 'pure investment bank' that bank did acquire a banking license after 2008.

I am calling every role in the front office of investment banks and investment banking divisions of megabanks 'investment bankers,' including research analysts, treasury sales people and the asset management division. I am using the term 'dealmaker' for both equity and debt capital markets bankers as well as corporate finance and mergers and acquisitions. Banks can differ slightly in the job titles they use, and the same is true of the exact delineations between back and middle office – some banks, for example, have put 'tax and legal' in a separate category.

All those nuances I have had to ignore as I had to leave out entirely the conflicts of interest between market making and prop trading, to the hidden fee structures in financial products, to tranches, shorting, leverages, shadow banking, risk-weighted capital buffers and fiat money. At the time of their interviews the regulators quoted in this book were working for the Financial Services Authority, which is now revamped and split into two parts, the Financial Conduct Authority and the Prudential Regulation Authority.

Goldman Sachs has denied that its employees refer to a particular set of clients as 'muppets' and Tony Blair's income at JP Morgan is an estimate by the *Financial Times*.

A final world about women and finance. The difference of opinion between young female interviewees who said they were adamantly opposed to quotas and their more experienced female colleagues who were in favour would have made for a great chapter. In the end I have decided to leave out a discussion of the glass ceiling since I believe the core of the problem with finance to be the structural conflicts and perverse incentives and not the gender of those responding to them. It is not at all inconceivable that on the whole men respond differently to the temptations that global finance offers them than women. That is probably what IMF president Christine Lagarde alluded to when she produced one of the best quotes I have come across during the research project: 'What if it had been Lehman Sisters?'

Acknowledgements

Over 200 insiders risked their job or severance package to give an interview. Thank you so much! I can only hope that in spite of all the constraints and limitations a book imposes I have done justice to your views and experiences.

Thank you also to all the insiders who while not giving an interview themselves joined the comment thread to offer their invaluable expertise. And thank you to the readers who helped spread the blog by sharing it through social media.

I am forever in Alan Rusbridger's debt for giving me this incredible opportunity. Thank you Kirsten Bloomhall, Charlotte Baxter and Nick Dastoor over at production, Philip Oltermann and David Shariatmadari at Comment, and Jan Thompson, Stephen Moss, Ian Katz, Matt McAllister, Wolfgang Blau, Chris Elliott, Chris Moran, Aditya Chakraborty, Madeleine Bunting and Keren Levy. Banking editor Jill Treanor was unfailingly kind to this Dutchman tramping all over her portfolio.

Thanks also to Hein Greven, Jan Maarten Slagter and Ewald Engelen in the Netherlands and Anni van Landeghem in Belgium. To my mother, Marc, Annedien and Sabine for their pieds à terre in the Netherlands, and for all their support and encouragement: Vera, Wouter, Jos, Lisa and Simon.

My agent Andrew Nurnberg was fantastic and so were Atlas Contact publishers in the Netherlands and Guardian-Faber in the UK; Laura Hassan's patience was superhuman, as was Lindsay Davies.' It is thanks to their editing skills that my Dunglish may have come to sound like actual English, at least here and there. While mistakes remain my sole responsibility, obviously, Amba Zeggen, Peter van Ees, Wouter Elsenburg in Amsterdam, Thomas Mosk in Frankfurt and a small army of anonymous helpers in London cleansed earlier versions of the manuscript of blunders that can still keep me awake at night. Toon van de Put was as marvellous a sub-editor as ever.

Sometimes the acknowledgements in a book like this conclude with a coded apology: sorry that I was emotionally and physically unavailable for the past year and a half but . . . look at the book Daddy has written! I genuinely hope that this time such an apology is not necessary.

Index

TK

About the Author

JORIS LUYENDIJK is a journalist and former writer of the *Guardian*'s banking blog. An anthropologist by training, he lives in London.